SAMSON X-FILE

"For My thoughts are not your thoughts, Nor are your ways My ways," declares the LORD. "For as the heavens are higher than the earth, so are My ways higher than your ways And My thoughts than your thoughts."

Isaiah 55:8, 9, NASB

ALSO WRITTEN BY RUTHVEN J. ROY

Unshakeable Kingdom
Position Yourself for Success
The Explosive Power of Network Discipling
Imitating God: The Amazing Secret of Living His Life
Born Again: How to Maximize Your New life in Christ

SAMSON X-FILE

WHAT YOU WERE NEVER TOLD

Ruthven J. Roy

Rehoboth
Publishing

Samson X-file: *What You Were Never Told*
Copyright © 2008, 2010, 2013 by Ruthven J. Roy

ISBN: Paperback   978-0-9717853-2-8

All rights reserved. No part of this book may be reproduced or transmitted in any form or by any means without written permission the publisher.

Unless otherwise indicated, Bible quotations are taken from the *New American Standard Bible,* © 1960, 1962, 1963, 1968, 1971, 1972, 1973, 1975, 1977, by The Lockman Foundation. Used by permission.
Scripture quotations marked (KJV) are taken from *The Authorized King James Version,* © 1975 by Thomas Nelson Inc., Publishers.
Verses marked (NRSV) are taken from the *New Revised Standard Version,* © 1989, by Division of Christian Education of the National Council of the Churches of Christ in the United States of America. Verses marked (AMP) are taken from *The Amplified Bible,* © 1987, by The Lockman Foundation. Used by permission.

Printed in the United States of America.

Rehoboth Publishing, LLC
P.O. Box 33
Berrien Springs, MI 49103

For additional copies of this book or for author speaking engagements write to:

ruthvenroy@gmail.com, or visit www.rehobothpublishing.com, or www.networkdiscipling.org

In Celebration of:

God's Providence and Purpose;
His Eternal Power and Godhead

Acknowledgments

    The writing of this volume was as distant from my mind as the East is from the West. If it were left to me, it would not have been written. I must therefore render due diligence to the One who initiated and orchestrated the unfolding of this entire manuscript—that is, God the Holy Spirit. Had it not been for His daily revelation and direction, I could not, by any stretch of my imagination, produce this very insightful work. Therefore, the Holy Spirit, and He alone, deserves all the credit for opening the Samson X-file to display the mysterious providence and majesty of God Almighty. To Him I give ALL the glory, honor, dominion and power!

    Additionally, I wish to acknowledge the valuable contributions of a few other people who assisted in the writing of this Samson project: Lyris, my wife, for her patient understanding and honest, critical evaluation of my work; my sisters, Ingrid McCarthy and Verlene Cromwell, for their constant support and kind encouragement; and Marilyn Bell-Joseph and Victoria Elder, for their quality editorial work and timely suggestions that helped make the manuscript a document worth reading.

CONTENTS

Preface 13

Foreword 15

Introduction 17

1. CHOSEN BEFORE BIRTH 29

2. DISOBEDIENT SON OR FEARLESS
   SERVANT? 43

3. UNDER THE INFLUENCE 69

4. DANCING WITH FOXES 79

5. FOR GOD, WIFE, AND COUNTRY 89

6. GOD'S ARMY OF ONE 99

7. PHILISTINE ADDICTION OR PUZZLING
   PROVIDENCE? 113

8. DEALING WITH DESTINY 141

9. REMEMBERING SAMSON 151

Preface

This book had to be written, not because I wanted to write it—it was never a part of my present or future writing agenda—but because God moved me very strongly so to do. For me, this was a most unusual experience because I have read the story of Samson many times over; but I have never encountered the truths that the Spirit of God revealed to me on this particular occasion.

It all started as a matter of course (at least, so I thought), as I made my way through the Bible, book after book, during my daily devotion. As I came to the book of Judges, and began studying the life of Samson, I could not get past the fourth verse of chapter 14. The verse reads: *"However, his father and mother did not know that it was of the LORD, for He was seeking an occasion against the Philistines."* For the very first time, the reality of this verse grabbed my attention and would not let go. Day after day, the Spirit of God beckoned me to fresh insights and revelations into a story I thought I knew so well. I was surprisingly very mistaken.

Thus began my eye-opening journey into the life of one of my childhood heroes, seen primarily through the window of God's sovereign will and providence, and not merely from the prevailing standpoint of Samson's actions. Suddenly, the over-arching presence of the God behind Samson transcended all the events of his battle-scarred life, filling me with not only a new vision of the Almighty, but also a fresh, jaw-dropping appreciation for the faith and courage of my hero.

I believe that you will be amazed, as I was, when you encounter the awesome majesty, power and wisdom of the Almighty in this real life drama that has been veiled in the sea of human suspicion for many centuries. This volume will challenge your preconceptions concerning this judge of Israel, as the mysterious purpose of God emerges out of every scene in the champion's life.

However, I trust that you will also experience, as I have, a new sense of hope with regard to all the situations in your life, as you become more keenly aware of the guiding presence of your all-seeing, all-knowing, loving Father. Moreover, I pray that you will be greatly blessed as you respond to the challenge called forth from the pages of this book.

- R. J. R

Foreword

Everyone has a childhood hero, from Little Red Riding Hood to Jesus of Nazareth, and all those in between. These heroes emerge from every walk of life and have made their indelible imprints on the minds of countless youngsters. However, the images and thoughts we have pertaining to our childhood heroes often change as we grow into adulthood. Some of these heroes often appear to be larger than life, and their impact on our lives continues to grow with the passing of the years, as our knowledge and understanding of them continue to expand.

In this inspirational landmark, Dr. Roy reveals how his childhood view of one of his heroes, Samson, which pervaded most of his adult life, suddenly took a turn for the best. He discovered that what he regarded as major flaws in Samson's character, were really evidences of an uncommon, one-of-a kind faith in the God who gave birth to him (Samson).

- M. D. C

Introduction

"Therefore I speak to them in parables; because while <u>seeing they do not see</u>, and <u>while hearing they do not hear, nor do they understand</u>. ¹⁴"In their case the prophecy of Isaiah is being fulfilled, which says, '<u>YOU WILL KEEP ON HEARING, BUT WILL NOT UNDERSTAND; YOU WILL KEEP ON SEEING, BUT WILL NOT PERCEIVE</u>;

¹⁵<u>FOR THE HEART OF THIS PEOPLE HAS BECOME DULL</u>, AND WITH THEIR EARS THEY SCARCELY HEAR, AND THEY HAVE CLOSED THEIR EYES, LEST THEY <u>SHOULD SEE WITH THEIR EYES, HEAR WITH THEIR EARS, AND UNDERSTAND WITH THEIR HEART AND RETURN, AND I SHOULD HEAL THEM</u>.'

¹⁶"But <u>blessed are your eyes, because they see; and your ears, because they hear</u>. ¹⁷"For truly I

INTRODUCTION

say to you that <u>many prophets and righteous men desired to see what you see, and did not see it, and to hear what you hear, and did not hear it.</u>"

Matthew 13:13-17

When Seeing is not Believing

From earliest childhood, we are taught to believe what we see with our eyes, touch with our hands, taste with our tongues, smell with our noses and hear with our ears—in short, believe whatever enters our minds through the avenues of our five senses. Because of this pre-conditioning, little children, and even adults, are often taken aback whenever they witness stellar performances, by very creative artistes and magicians that simply defy comprehension. However, as an informed adult, I have now come to understand and believe that we can educate our minds to change the way in which we perceive what is real. This ability, I believe, is what provides the foundation for developing various types of biases or prejudicial attitudes towards people, information, and situations. Daily, we see these attitudes displayed in race relations, media presentations, sports and games analyses, political speeches by crafty spin-doctors, or individuals who seek to veil the truth about anything for the purpose of gaining some personal advantage.

This was the type of situation that Jesus faced when He came preaching the gospel of the kingdom to the nation of Israel. The Jewish leadership had already formed their opinion of the Messiah before He actually arrived, and had taught the people to prepare for the fictitious coronation of a religio-political king. Thus, when God's Messiah did appear, and the Truth was manifested in person and the proclaimed Word before the nation, the leaders and people did not believe the witness He bore.

Therefore, Jesus chose to speak to the people in parables, *"because while <u>seeing they [did] not see</u>, and <u>while hearing they [did] not hear</u>, <u>nor [did] they understand</u>"* (Matthew 13:13). Because their spirits were disconnected from the life of God, the leaders of Israel had educated their minds, and those of the Jewish masses, to reject the Messiah and the truth He proclaimed about the kingdom of heaven. It was certainly not to their religious and political advantage or ambition to accept either.

Consequently, Christ further declared, in the words of the prophet Isaiah, that the *"heart [spiritual core] of this people has become dull [insensitive], and with their ears they scarcely hear, and they have closed their eyes [of their mind or understanding] lest they should see with their eyes, hear with their ears, and understand with their heart and return, and I should heal them"* (Matthew 13:15, parenthesis mine).

Here is represented the ultimate example of when seeing is not believing. When once a person's spirit is divorced from the life of God it is impossible for that individual to discern or comprehend spiritual things unless he/she has been regenerated (quicken from the "dead,"

Ephesians 2:1) from above by the Holy Spirit. In this regard, Jesus told Nicodemus: *"That which is born of the flesh is flesh, and that which is born of the Spirit is spirit"* (John 3:6). The apostle Paul clearly agreed with this when he stated:

> *Now we have received not <u>the spirit of the world</u>, but <u>the Spirit who is from God</u>, that we might know the things freely given to us by God, ¹³which things we also speak, not in words taught by human wisdom, but in those taught by the Spirit, combining spiritual thoughts with spiritual words. ¹⁴But <u>a natural man</u> does not accept the things of the Spirit of God; <u>for they are foolishness to him</u>, and <u>he cannot understand them</u>, <u>because they are spiritually appraised</u>.*
>
> 1 Corinthians 2:12-14

The natural man refers not only to the unregenerated sinner, but also to the "born again" person who is still dominated by his/her fleshly thought-life and fallen world-view. Such a person is quite capable of being very religious (like the scribe and Pharisees were), astute in biblical knowledge, zealous in good works, but yet not controlled by the Spirit from above.

There is a world of difference between human wisdom (worldly or religious intellectualism) and the wisdom that comes from above, each bearing the fruit of the tree that gave birth to it—either of Life unto life or death unto death. James explains that human wisdom is envious, selfish, arrogant, unspiritual and devilish, always leading to disorder and every imaginable form of evil; but the wisdom from above, he says, is first of all pure; then peace-loving, considerate, submissive, full of mercy and good fruit, impartial and sincere (James 3:14-17).

So how do we see when we read the Word of God? The Bible says in 1 Corinthians 13:12 that presently, *"we see through a glass darkly."* Our eyes and our ears are virtual windows and doors to our minds. Paul's description suggests that the windows of our eyes are very cloudy, dark, or opaque, obscuring our vision. Our windows are very cloudy because they reflect the condition of our spirit and mind.

Depending on the state of our minds, our vision could be very misty-grey, but never completely clear because of the weakness of our flesh. The real "truth," then, is that we tend to see with our minds, and not so much our eyes. We really see *through* our eyes, rather than *with* them. This is the reason a person could be present in body in a room and yet go places, see things, hear sounds and have experiences (good and bad) in his/her mind.

We often refer to this phenomenon as "spacing out," being "absent-minded," or even fantasizing. This ability of the mind to see and hear, and even taste, feel and smell things without having them present, renders us very susceptible to making mistakes in our judgment of reality. I am afraid that this extends to every area of our existence, for when our spirits are compromised through infection on account of our flesh, our minds, along with all our senses, become distorted as well.

How strikingly relevant and powerful are the words of the wise man, Solomon, who wrote: *Watch over your heart [spirit and mind] with all diligence, for from it flow the springs of life* (Proverbs 4:23). Jesus addressed the same idea when He was explaining the matter of personal defilement to His disciples:

> *"For from within, out of the heart of men, proceed the evil thoughts, fornications, thefts, murders, adulteries, ^{22}deeds of coveting and wickedness, as well as deceit, sensuality, envy, slander, pride and foolishness.*

Mark 7:21, 22

The word heart, in both these scriptures, refers to the spiritual core or the moral center of a person. This means more than just the mind (the organ of intellect, emotions and will), but also includes the spirit or motive force (the seat of conscience, intuition and divine communion) that drives the mind as well. Notice that Jesus' enumeration of sins is the direct product of the "*base and evil thoughts*" that proceed from the core of the man, and not the blood-pumping organ in the chest cavity. In the gospel of Matthew, Jesus says:

> "... for out of the abundance of the heart [spirit] the mouth speaketh. A good man out of the good treasure of his heart bringeth forth good things: and an evil man out of the evil treasure of his heart bringeth forth evil things."
>
> Matthew 12:34, KJV

The contents (treasure or deposits, good or bad) of a person's spirit and mind determine what proceeds from his/her mouth and influence what flows from his/her life. Whatever we sow into our spirit (good or evil) will decide our life's harvest—temporal and eternal. All these words of Jesus give credible weight to the counsel of Solomon, which tells us to stand guard over our spirit for it is the production center of whatever happens in our lives (Proverb 4:23). The child of God should diligently watch over his/her spirit self, by daily renewing his/her mind through the implantation of the precious seed of the Word of God (Luke 8:11), so that he/she may personally ascertain and confirm the good, acceptable and perfect will of the Almighty (Romans 12:2).

This is so appropriate and so right for us since our thoughts, influenced by our spiritual or carnal self, color what we see and how we relate to everything in our life; and these are of even greater consequence in our walk with God. Someone has wisely and correctly stated that we tend to see things, not as they are, but as we are. As a complement to this, Robert (Bob) Leslie said that a person's attitude is his/her mind's paintbrush; it can color any situation.[1]

Mind over Matter

This book is about my reflection on how my mental framework distorted my understanding of the story of the favorite bible character of my childhood (Samson), and how God, through His Spirit, gave me a fresh revelation of His sovereignty and faithfulness that left me completely dumbfounded, with a hunger for a deeper, broader, knowledge of Him. Therefore, it is my purpose, through this volume, to bring perspective and balance to the story of a servant of God who has been wrongly judged by many who profess Christ's name. I shall also use the biblical record to portray the truth about this valiant hero of faith. Just as there are two sides to every coin, there is the other side to this Samson saga that needs to be told.

I believe that I am not alone in saying that my former conclusions about Samson—that he was a very strong man with weak moral reins, a disobedient, self-willed spirit, and a volatile, uncontrollable temper—were, wholly or partly, the result of the perpetuation of a story that was related to me in my childhood, reinforced through my teenage viewing of the silver-screen production of "Samson and Delilah," and confirmed by the accounts of the saga that were told to me at my introduction to Christianity.

Here is a very classic example of this phenomenon:

How many Christians are going about life with the accepted belief that Delilah was the wife of Samson, when the Bible teaches something completely different? Unfortunately, for many years I believed this. I have told the Samson story many times over with that foregone conclusion. However, I was always haunted by the thought that such conclusions did not align with the enviable accolades accorded this 'rebellious' youth in God's hall of faith in the eleventh chapter of the book of Hebrews.

It is nothing short of amazing to see how a prevailing mental picture of an idea or storyline can distort what we see and read. Despite my years of theological training, I failed to see and to grasp the fascinating truths that God was seeking to teach me about Himself and His servant Samson. Very early in my experience as an author, I became embarrassingly aware of my folly of trying to be the editor of my own manuscripts. Regardless of how carefully I read them, I was not able to see all the typographical errors and poor grammatical constructions that were discovered by my independent readers. Independent editors bring a fresh pair of eyes and a mind that is not tainted by the personal biases of the author. It soon became very clear to me that instead of reading every word that I had written, I was subconsciously reviewing the thoughts and ideas that were already imbedded in my mind, skipping over, even omitting, words as I eagerly went along.

I am afraid that the same thing happens when I read the Bible. Consequently, I have to be painstakingly careful to read every word with an "open mind" and let the Spirit and the Word inform my seeing and my processing of the message that God intends for me to receive. It is very easy for us to allow our own perspectives—be they personal, denominational, organizational or otherwise—to color what we see whenever we read the Word of God. It is for this reason we must always approach the scriptures, not as an expert or an investigator seeking to confirm what we already believe, but as a learner, so that God can reveal Himself and His purpose to us.

The Almighty cautions us: *"Be still and know that I am God . . ."* (Psalm 46:10). In other words, quiet your mind and soul before Him, and hold the reins on your judgments; and God will declare His ways and purposes to you. Job asked the rhetorical questions: *"Canst thou by searching find out God? Canst thou find out the Almighty unto perfection?"* (Job 11:7, KJV). The implied answer to these questions is most certainly no. We simply cannot understand the Almighty or His purpose by mere intellectual investigation and logical reasoning; God must reveal both of these transcendent verities to us, and without such revelation, our view of truth and reality would be woefully distorted.

I want to encourage you, the readers of this volume, to first prayerfully and "open-mindedly" go through the entire story of Samson, found in Judges 13-16, before reading the contents of this book; and may the Spirit of God do for you what He did for me—reveal the other side of this amazing saga.

Notes:

1. Quotes from Bob Leslie, at www.angelfire.com/ok/freshenglish/goodquotes.html

1

CHOSEN BEFORE BIRTH

There was a certain man of Zorah, of the family of the Danites, whose name was Manoah; and his wife was barren and had borne no children. ³Then <u>the angel of the LORD</u> appeared to the woman and said to her, "Behold now, you are barren and have borne no children, but you shall conceive and give birth to a son.

⁴"Now therefore, be careful not to drink wine or strong drink, nor eat any unclean thing. ⁵"<u>For behold, you shall conceive and give birth to a son, and no razor shall come upon his head, for the boy shall be a Nazirite to God from the womb</u>; and he shall begin to deliver Israel from the hands of the Philistines."

⁶Then the woman came and told her husband, saying, "A man of God came to me

> *and his appearance was like the appearance of the angel of God, very awesome. And I did not ask him where he came from, nor did he tell me his name.* ⁷*"But he said to me, 'Behold, you shall conceive and give birth to a son, and now you shall not drink wine or strong drink nor eat any unclean thing, <u>for the boy shall be a Nazirite to God from the womb to the day of his death.</u>'"*

Judges 13:2-7

The very first thing we observe as we begin reading the Samson saga is his ancestry. Manoah, Samson's father, was a descendant from the tribe of Dan, son of Jacob, the father of all Israel, and Bilhah, Rachel's maid. The writer of the book of Judges did not mention the name of Manoah's wife, but did indicate that she was unable to bear children—a "misfortune" that was a part of his ancestral history. Both Sarah, Manoah's ancestral grandmother, and Rachel, the wife of one of his ancestral grandfathers, were barren.

However, what was considered a misfortune, or even a curse, among the people of early Bible times was really a divine opportunity for the outworking of God's mysterious purpose. As it was for Sarah, Abraham's wife (Genesis 18:1-15), so it was for the wife of Manoah. The angel of the Lord appeared to her and told her that her womb would be opened and she was going to give birth to a son (Judges 13:3).

> "Now therefore, be careful not to drink wine or strong drink, nor eat any unclean thing. For behold, you shall conceive and give birth to a son, and no razor shall come upon his head, for the boy shall be a Nazirite to God from the womb; and he shall begin to deliver Israel from the hands of the Philistines."
>
> Judges 13:4, 5

We know now, as Manoah and his wife found out later, that the angel who declared the good news of the deliverer's birth was the Lord, Himself. When the wife of Manoah relayed to him all that the angel had said to her, this God-fearing father-to-be did what every expectant parent ought to do—entreat the Lord for wisdom and guidance in raising the unborn child. Manoah prayed:

> "O Lord, please let the man of God whom You have sent come to us again that he may teach us what to do for the boy who is to be born."
>
> Judges 13:8

Such a simple, earnest prayer our heavenly Father will always answer—either directly or by some other means of His choosing—for it is in direct accordance with

His divine will. James instructs us: *"But if any of you lacks wisdom, let him ask of God, who gives to all generously and without reproach, and it will be given to him"* (James 1:5). Thus, when the man of God returned, in answer to the expectant father's prayer, Manoah opened the conversation with a question: *"Are you the man of God who spoke to the woman?"* This question suggests that Manoah was not only interested in authenticating his wife's story, but also wanted to certify that he was receiving the same information from the primary, and not a secondary, source.

Separated For War

Once Manoah authenticated his source, whom, till then, he did not fully recognize, he proceeded to ask his primary question. Now that you have given us this marvelous news and we are going to have this miracle son, what shall be the mode of life and vocation of this boy (Judges 13:12)? In other words, what is the real (or divine) purpose of this child's life? Again, this is a very important question that every expectant parent should be asking our benevolent, Father in heaven. Why? Because every child born into this world is a miraculous gift of God, ordained and endowed for some appointed purpose. The psalmist David reminds us of this very fact in speaking of his own existence and purpose.

For <u>You formed my inward parts</u>; <u>You wove</u>

<u>me in my mother's womb</u>. <u>*¹⁴I will give thanks to You, for I am fearfully and wonderfully made;*</u> *Wonderful are Your works, And my soul knows it very well.* <u>*¹⁵My frame was not hidden from You, when I was made in secret,*</u> *And skillfully wrought in the depths of the earth;* <u>*¹⁶Your eyes have seen my unformed substance; And in Your book were all written The days that were ordained for me, when as yet there was not one of them.*</u>

Psalm 139:13-16

These are very deep, powerful thoughts and expressions regarding human life. Once conception takes place, the mystery of God begins its appointed operation and never stops until that fetus, which—if accorded its divine right—becomes a human being, eventually dies. The purpose of every life is carefully chronicled in God's book of remembrance, and if we live in cooperation with the will of heaven, the days that were ordained for us will be certainly fulfilled. I believe that if parents were more knowledgeable and cognizant of these sacred issues regarding the existence and life of their children, they would be more prayerful (not just careful) regarding the advice and direction they give them in choosing their career paths and life's dreams.

Obviously, Manoah wanted to pursue God's purpose for his unborn son. As such, he diligently sought information and guidance from the heavenly visitor. In answer to Manoah's inquiry, the angel of the Lord repeated the announcement and instructions he gave to the expectant mother. These comprised two parts. The first had to do with the couple's parental obligations in raising the child, and the second focused on his life's purpose and mission.

The angel specifically instructed the woman: *"be careful not to drink wine or strong drink, nor eat any unclean thing . . . and no razor shall come upon his head, for the boy shall be a Nazirite unto God from the womb to the day of his death"* (verses 5, 7). Implied in these instructions is the very cogent life principle that a parent's diet and lifestyle have a direct influence on the temperament and behavior of their children; for God's immutable law of procreation—*every seed producing after its kind* (Genesis 1:11, 12)—will continue to operate in every life-form until the end of time.

Although the call to abstinence from wine and strong drink was given to the woman, it is reasonable to believe that Manoah also accepted that responsibility to ensure that his son would be raised in an environment that was both conducive and compatible to the life for which this boy was divinely appointed to live.

Quality childrearing is the responsibility of both parents. Both must work harmoniously together, to provide their children with the best possible advantages and opportunities to become balanced, productive citizens in the world, and for the kingdom of God. Sad to say, this is not what pertains in a large number of families today; for in many instances, this responsibility falls upon the shoulders of single moms and dads, who are doing what they consider necessary to rear their children.

Essentially, these grateful parents were enjoined by God to commit themselves to His purpose in giving them a son, who was divinely appointed to be a Nazirite to Himself from the womb to the tomb. Accordingly, they covenanted to support this child in God's requirement of him to (1) abstain from wine or strong drink; (2) consume absolutely nothing that was produced from the fruit of the vine, including the skin or seed of the grape; (3) allow the locks of the hair of his head to grow long, for no razor was ever to touch his head; and (4) avoid any contact with a dead person.[1]

It is also very important to note that this boy was to be a Nazirite, separated for war; for he was to <u>*begin* to *deliver Israel from the hands of the Philistines*</u> (Judges 13:5, emphasis mine). The purpose and mission of Samson's life was determined by God before the warrior was even born.

Divine Endorsement

The response of a grateful heart is often demonstrated in one's willingness to give back. Manoah was so overjoyed to be honored by the presence and the good tidings of the man of God that he was willing to prepare a sumptuous fellowship spread. However, the divine messenger courteously informed Manoah that his visit was strictly for business, and that a burnt offering to the Lord would be a more appropriate gesture of his gratitude and thanksgiving.

Still thinking that he was dealing with a man of God, Manoah pressed him for his name so that he could repay his kindness to his household. The angel responded with a question of his own: *"Why do you ask my name, seeing that it is wonderful"* (Judges 13:18)? By this response, the heavenly visitor gave a hint to Manoah of who he really was, but the over-excited father-to-be did not recognize or understand it.

The cognate Hebrew word the angel used for "wonderful" (***peli*** – a miracle or wonder or act of God), was the same word used in the Messianic prophecy (Isaiah 9:6) to describe the work of Jesus. This signifies that Manoah's guest of honor was none other than the Lord, Himself, and it was immediately confirmed as soon as Manoah offered his sacrifice to God; for *the angel of the Lord ascended in the flame of the altar* (Judges 13:20). This riveting, spectacular phenomenon momentarily floored Manoah and his wife, and they instantly recognized that their benevolent guest was not a man of God after all, but God, Himself (vv. 21-22).

The significance of the Christ ascending in the flames of Manoah's sacrifice was indicative of God's acceptance of not only the humble couple's offering, but also of His covenanting[2] with them. This covenant guaranteed that their unborn son would be heaven's chosen, consecrated vessel to initiate Israel's deliverance from the dominion of the Philistines. In so doing, God had placed His divine signet on the birth and mission of Samson.

When the child was born, his mother called him Samson, which literally means "of the sun." There is no viable record of why she chose that name. It could possibly be linked to the lingering influence of the heathen cultures that surrounded Israel, which accorded great respect to the sun deity; but no one knows for certain.

Nevertheless, as the time drew near for the purpose of God to be unfurled, the Spirit of Jehovah began to agitate Samson, driving him toward His appointed destiny. Thus began the most intriguing journey of one of the most misunderstood servants of God; but one who, nevertheless, defied those odds and found eternal favor with the One who personally ordained his life and his existence.

Samson and You

"... *I shall ... <u>be like any other man</u>.*"

Judges 16:7, 11, 13, 16

Unmasking the Error

For most of my life I was of the opinion that Samson was a very muscular, giant of a man, way above the head and shoulder of the average man of his time. After a very careful review of his story, I now realize that I was in love with my childhood fantasy and a silver screen action figure. How many thousands (maybe millions) still believe as I did, and probably for the very same reasons.

However, scripture gives absolutely no indication that Samson was an exploded version of a "Mr. Universe" or the "Incredible Hulk"—with rock-hard muscles, massive legs, broad back and bulging chest. That's a silver screen version of the truth. God did not (and does not) need all that packaging to display his strength and power in a mere man. Samson's strength was never in his physical structure or his hair, but in his relationship with his God; and the Bible portrays that power as having been visible only when the Spirit of God rushed upon him (Judges 14:6, 19; 15:14; 16:28-30).

Moreover, Samson, himself, repeatedly made reference to his equality with other men, when he flirted with Delilah over the real secret of his strength. These references, found in Judges 16:7, 11, 13, 16, essentially said that if the secret of his strength (God, not physique or muscle) was taken away, he would be like every other man. This, to me, is the clue for unmasking the error that Samson had some physical advantage over and above the other men of his time. His superiority was the result of nothing else than his covenant relationship with His God, who had given birth to him for a specific divine purpose. Apart from this, Samson was like any other man of his time.

What does this mean for you and me? It means that Samson, like Elijah, was a man subject to like passions as we are (James 5:17), yet, through his covenant relationship with God, was able to accomplish great exploits for the glory of His name. It means that regardless of our size, sex, shape, ethnicity, family history, or any other human component, you and I can achieve remarkable things for the glory of God through our covenant relationship with Christ. Jesus said that we will do greater works than He did because He was going to the Father on our behalf (John 14:12). Standing firmly on this promise, the apostle Paul declared: "*I can do everything through Him who gives me strength*" (Philippians 4:13).

The story of Samson is not so much the story of his supernatural strength as it is the story of the sovereignty of God's purpose in the life of a consecrated vessel. Hence, finding God's purpose for your life through a covenant relationship with Him is the secret to victorious living, as it was the secret to Samson's mysterious strength.

Notes:

1. See Numbers 6:2-21 for a full account of the vow of a Nazirite. Also note that the vow could have been taken for a period of time, or for the entire length of a person's life.
2. The act of Christ ascending in the flames that consumed the pieces of Manoah's offering was the equivalent of God (the smoking oven and the flaming torch) passing between the pieces of Abraham's sacrifice (Genesis 15:1-18) when He cut His covenant with His servant.

Please observe that in both of these accounts, that it was God, and not man, who was cutting the covenant, and placing Himself on the line for their fulfillment.

MY THOUGHTS

CHOSEN BEFORE BIRTH

2

DISOBEDIENT SON OR FEARLESS SERVANT?

Once Samson went down to Timnah, and at Timnah he saw a Philistine woman. ²Then he came up, and told his father and mother, "I saw a Philistine woman at Timnah; now get her for me as my wife." ³But his father and mother said to him, "Is there not a woman among your kin, or among all our people, that you must go to take a wife from among the uncircumcised Philistines?" But Samson said to his father, "Get her for me, because she pleases me."

⁴<u>His father and mother did not know that this was from the LORD; for he was seeking a pretext to act against the Philistines</u>. At that time the Philistines had dominion over Israel.

⁵Then Samson went down with his father

and mother to Timnah. When he came to the vineyards of Timnah, suddenly a young lion roared at him. <u>⁶The spirit of the LORD rushed on him</u>, and he tore the lion apart barehanded as one might tear apart a kid. <u>But he did not tell his father or his mother what he had done</u>.

Judges 14:1-6, NRSV

Driven

I believe that it is quite appropriate and necessary to begin this chapter with a few forthright questions that, I am convinced, would lead us into the very heart of the Samson saga. Here we go: What would cause a young man, who was filled with the Spirit of God from the womb, raised a Nazirite all his life, and lovingly nurtured and blessed by God, to suddenly "forsake" such a rich heritage and choose a path that appeared out of character with his spiritual upbringing and way of life? Did Samson just wake one morning and decide that it was time for him to get a wife; to go down to Timnah and find a daughter of the Philistines instead of one from among his own people? What really happened here?

It seems rather obvious that the last verse of chapter 13 appears to be setting the stage for whatever was going to happen next in Samson's life. Although we do not know the exact timing of all the events in this intriguing saga—since they occurred over a period of 20 years—it would appear that the writer of this intriguing story is clearly trying to make a connection between Samson's spiritual preparation and the premier episode of his electrifying adventure.

The Bible says: *And the Spirit of the LORD <u>began to stir him</u> in Mahaneh-dan, between Zorah and Eshtaol* (Judges 13:25). The most logical questions to ask after reading this verse would be: "Why was the Spirit beginning to stir Samson?" "What was the Spirit stirring Samson to do?" I believe that the answers to both of these questions can be found in the chapter immediately following them.

This chapter opens with Samson taking decisive action that went "against the grain" of his spiritual and cultural upbringing. I believe that the Spirit of God was beginning to stir Samson because the fullness of time had come for God to make manifest the purpose for which He birthed His servant. It is also reasonable to believe that the phrase "began to stir" infers to both Samson's discovery of his supernatural strength and ability, and his natural desire for a life companion, since both were in harmony with God's plan.

Therefore, it is quite appropriate to ask: "Why would the Spirit drive Samson to marry an unbeliever?" For the very same reason the Spirit drove Christ to the wilderness to be tempted of the Devil (Matthew 4:1), or God would tell His prophet to marry a temple prostitute (Hosea 1:1-3)—that is, to fulfill God's purpose for which they were born.

Samson was not, in any way, psychotic, obstinate, rebellious or selfish, as many Christian storytellers, teachers and writers may suggest. He was driven!—driven by the same Spirit that began to stir him at Mahaneh-dan, calling him to his appointed destiny.

What Parents and Others Don't Know

His father and mother did not know that this was from the LORD; for he was seeking a pretext to act against the Philistines. At that time the Philistines had dominion over Israel.

Judges 14:4, NRSV

Unbeknown to his parents and anyone else, Samson sets off to Timnah to begin his mission assignment. The author does not fill in all the necessary behind-the-scene details to satisfy our query of Samson's motives; he simply states that Samson saw a daughter of the Philistines and he returned to his parents with a very firm demand—absolutely no questions asked. *"I saw a woman in Timnah, one of the daughters of the Philistines; now therefore, get her for me as a wife"* (Judges 14:2).

One can only imagine the utter consternation and horror of the old couple who had done their very best to raise their son after God's order. Instinctively, Samson's parents met his request with the very reasonable question: *"Is there no woman among the daughters of your relatives, or among all our people, that you go to take a wife from the uncircumcised Philistines?"* But Samson paid absolutely no attention to the request. He did not even give a reason for his seemingly obdurate, inflexible demand: *"Get her for me, for she looks good to me"* (v. 3).

Many Christian teachers and leaders have had their field days with Samson's forthright demand imposed on his parents, labeling the rising warrior as selfish, unreasonable, unthankful, and licentious, among other things. However, in their rush to judgment, they fail to diligently inquire about what was responsible for this abrupt change in attitude (for it was abrupt) of this otherwise spirit-filled young man. Why would this youth suddenly decide to treat his parents this way?

I am convinced that Samson meant no disrespect toward his God-fearing parents, because he loved them. However, sometimes it is painfully difficult (nearing impossible) to explain to one's parents and others what God is doing in one's life, or the path He is calling one to tread. Ultimately, God alone knows the path we take when He tries us to bring us forth as gold (Job 23:10).

Samson's parents were probably thinking on the side of "logic" and the consequence of disobedience, just as we often do. On the other hand, Samson was probably thinking on the side of "purpose" and the consequence of obedience. How could he explain to his aged parents, whose minds were bent on following the letter of God's command against intermarriage with the heathen nations that surrounded them, what God was calling him to do?

This God-warrior was pursuing a course of action that went against the grain of their mind-set, and it was very difficult, even impossible, for him to put the new wine of God's supreme purpose in the brittle wineskins of their logical, "black and white" mentality. Consequently, Samson kept his request and remarks extremely brief, but also very firm. His heart was the hiding place for a divine secret known only to God and himself. The Bible says in Judges 14:4:

> *His father and mother did not know that <u>this</u> was from the LORD for He was seeking a pretext to act against the Philistines.*
>
> Judges 14:4, NRSV

What was that "this" that Samson's parents did not know? Most distinctly it was Samson's unswerving desire to marry a daughter of the Philistines. It is very important to see here that God, not Samson or his parents, was responsible for choosing the pretext for His intended purpose to destroy the Philistines. This one verse of scripture (Judges 14:4) is the *X-file* of the entire Samson saga, for it contains the invisible, mysterious and very powerful *X-Factor* (God) behind the warrior's misunderstood life and disconcerting behavior.

In a very similar way, it was God who chose the context for Joshua and Israel to wage war with the kings of the cities which occupied the promise land. The Bible says

> *. . . it was <u>of the LORD</u> to harden their hearts, to meet Israel in battle in order that he might utterly destroy them, that they might receive no mercy, but that he might destroy them . . .*
>
> Joshua 11:20

The above scripture uses the very same phrase (*of the Lord*) that formed the pre-condition for God's destruction of the Philistines at the hand of His servant, Samson. Here again, it was God, not Joshua, Israel or the kings of Canaan, who initiated and established the prevailing conditions that incited the nations of Canaan to make war with the sons of Israel.

In the New Testament, we are another very pointed example of God's providence at work. The Word of God says that before Joseph and Mary became sexually intimate, she was found with child *of the Holy Ghost* (Matthew 1:18). In my humble estimate, *of the Lord* and *of the Holy Ghost* amount to one and the same, for God is the great Author in both cases.

Accordingly, if *of the Lord* does not really mean *of the Lord*, but only an attribution to His sovereignty, according to some theologians; then *of the Holy Ghost* does not really mean that the child, Jesus, whom the Virgin Mary carried within her womb, was really from the Holy Ghost. It would mean that the immaculate conception of baby Jesus was only an attribution to the Holy Ghost, not a direct action on His part; and, therefore, calls into question Mary's claim to be a chaste virgin.

Where does such a preposterous argument leave us? It leaves us with a "juicy," nativity scandal about a messianic imposter, and a spurious, hopeless gospel. I praise the God of heaven that this is not the case! I would rather believe the Bible for what it says about God than to allow my human logic to invent a reason aimed at justifying the actions of the Almighty.

I do not have to "defend" God, or what He says in His Word (what a crazy notion). God and His truth stand aloof far above the best, unimpeachable thoughts of men. The Great Jehovah alone is the King eternal, immortal, invisible and only wise God (1 Timothy 1:17, KJV); there is absolutely no searching of His understanding, and His ways are past finding out (Romans 11:33, KJV). It is He who declares:

> "For My thoughts are not your thoughts, nor are your ways My ways," declares the LORD. "For as the heavens are higher than the earth, so are My ways higher than your ways And My thoughts than your thoughts."
>
> Isaiah 55:8, 9

Clearly, Samson's parents had "better" plans for him, other than his choosing a wife from among the neighboring tribes of Israel. They were hoping that, at the "appropriate time," their son (really God's child) would choose a wife from among their own tribe or people. However, God had other plans for Samson unknown to them. Although the angel of the Lord (Jesus Christ) gave them specific instructions on how to raise their son, He did not tell them in specific terms the purpose for which the child was to be raised a Nazirite. This He kept a secret. Isn't it rather strange that Christ kept God's purpose hidden from Samson's parents? Quite so! But in the realm of the spirit, some things are better left unsaid when individuals are not ready (spiritually attuned) to receive them.

Misreading God's Command

Samson's decision must have grievously troubled his parents and flooded their minds with a host of unanswered questions: *Why is he doing this? What's happening to our son? Is he losing his mind? Who is he listening to* (of course, Samson was listening to "Someone" they could not see)? *What did we do wrong? What did we not do? How can we help him? Who else knows about what's going on with him? When will this all end?* After all, they knew what God had commanded, and Samson was choosing a path that appeared to be in direct opposition to that command. God had given Israel specific instruction regarding intermarriage with the people of the heathen nations they dispossessed from the promise land.

When the LORD your God brings you into the land where you are entering to possess it, and clears away many nations before you, the Hittites and the Girgashites and the Amorites and the Canaanites and the Perizzites and the Hivites and the Jebusites, seven nations greater and stronger than you, ²and when the LORD your God delivers them before you and you defeat them, then you shall utterly destroy them. You shall make no covenant with them and show no favor to them.

³Furthermore, <u>you shall not intermarry with them; you shall not give your daughters to their sons, nor shall you take their daughters for your sons.</u> <u>⁴For they will turn your sons away from following Me to serve other gods; then the anger of the LORD will be kindled against you and He will quickly destroy you.</u>

⁵But thus you shall do to them: you shall tear down their altars, and smash their sacred pillars, and hew down their Asherim, and burn their graven images with fire. ⁶For you are a holy people to the LORD your God; the LORD your God has chosen you to be a people for His own possession out of all the peoples who are on the face of the earth.

Deuteronomy 7:1-6

It is very important to notice the purpose behind God's command that prohibited intermarriage between Israel and the heathen nations: *"For they will turn your sons away from following Me to serve other gods; then the anger of the LORD will be kindled against you and He will quickly destroy you"* (verse 4). Consequently, Samson's parents had a very legitimate concern regarding their son's decision to marry a Philistine. However, what these well-meaning parents and many in Israel failed to realize was that they were only keeping the letter of the law while violating its spiritual intent.

The children of Israel were not yoked to the Philistines through formal marriages, but they were laying in bed with them through spiritual whoredom; for they were joined in worship to the heathen gods—Baal and the Ashtaroth, the gods of Aram, Sidon, Moab, Ammon, and the gods of the Philistines. His chosen people violated the very purpose for which God instructed them not to give their sons and daughters in marriage to the children of the heathen nations that surrounded them. Israel was not joined to the Philistines in the flesh, but the nation was yoked to the heathens in spirit; and Samson became a very vivid portrayal of their folly. God did not possess the hearts of His people as He did the heart of His servant Samson.

Then the sons of Israel again did evil in the sight of the LORD, served the Baals and the Ashtaroth, the gods of Aram, the gods of Sidon, the gods of Moab, the gods of the sons

> *of Ammon, and the gods of the Philistines;* <u>*thus they forsook the LORD and did not serve Him*</u>*. The anger of the LORD burned against Israel, and He sold them into the hands of the Philistines and into the hands of the sons of Ammon.*
>
> Judges 10:6

How many professed Christians today who tout the biblical teaching of not being unequally yoked with unbelievers (2 Corinthians 6:14-16) are following the same course as the children of Israel? While they exert painstaking efforts to maintain a safe distance from the ungodly in pursuance of this biblical injunction, they are bedfellows with the world in the worshipping of their gods—self, pleasure, wealth, fame, materialism, immorality, etc. Paul says in 2 Timothy 3:1-5:

> *But realize this, that in the last days difficult times will come. ²For men will be lovers of self, lovers of money, boastful, arrogant, revilers, disobedient to parents, ungrateful, unholy, ³unloving, irreconcilable, malicious gossips, without self-control, brutal, haters of good,*
>
> *⁴treacherous, reckless, conceited,* <u>*lovers of pleasure rather than lovers of God*</u>*, ⁵*<u>*holding to a form of godliness, although they have*</u>

denied its power; Avoid such men as these.

2 Timothy 3:1-5

Like Israel of old, many professing Christianity in these last days will expend all their efforts to maintain the letter of the God's commands, while violating the very spirit that the commands were given to preserve. They will hold to or profess an empty, powerless form of godliness and judge others by their vain standards.

Samson's parents failed to realize that Israel was already living in violation of the principle of God's command, and for her disobedience, He had allowed her sons and daughters to become the servants of the Philistines. Further, Manoah and his wife did not know that God birthed and raised Samson to be His medium to make war with the heathen nation, and to initiate Israel's deliverance from servitude.

The Almighty intended to use Samson's relationship with the Philistines as the instrument to destroy them for enslaving His people. Judges 14:4 forms the bedrock for everything that happened in Samson's life. It is this single verse (the *X-file*), out of the four chapters, that unlocks the confusion that surrounds the life of this great warrior.

His father and mother did not know that <u>this</u> was from the LORD for He was seeking a pretext to act against the Philistines.

Judges 14:4, NRSV

Disobeying to Obey

Was Samson really a disobedient son? Absolutely not! He was doing neither more, nor less, than what Jesus did when he left His earthly parents' side from following the crowd, and went to the temple to reason with the teachers and leaders of Israel (Luke 2:41-52). While Joseph and Mary knew that the son they were raising came directly from God, and even had some idea about His future, they were not acquainted with the path that He was ordained to tread.

There were many things about Jesus' life that God hid from Joseph and Mary, because He did not want humanity—parental instincts, with all their good intentions—to get in the way of His divine purpose. Twice, in the same chapter, scripture records Mary as pondering in her heart revelations concerning the mysterious life of her son. Once, in Luke 2:19, when she heard the declaration of the angelic hosts who were praising God after the birth of her son; and then again when she heard Jesus' response to her very discreet verbal chiding (Luke 2:49).

The scenario of this verbal exchange between Jesus and His earthly parents has some marked similarities to what occurred between Samson and his earthly parents when he returned from his visit to Timnah. Just as at the call (or stirring) of the Spirit, Samson went to Timnah (gentile territory) unknown to his parents, so it was that the boy Jesus left his parents' side and went to the temple unknown to them. Obviously influenced by her maternal anxiety, Mary tried to insinuate that Jesus had acted improperly by "sneaking" away from them to visit the temple. She voiced her displeasure by asking the question: *"Son, why hast thou dealt thus with us?* (Luke 2:48, KJV). Jesus responded with a gentle rebuke of His own, also in the form of a question: *"How is it that ye sought me? wist ye not that I must be about my Father's business?"*

When Samson's parents posed the question: *"Is there no woman among the daughters of your relatives, or among all our people, that you go to take a wife from the uncircumcised Philistines"* (Judges 14:3)? and Samson demanded: *"Get her for me, for she looks good to me;"* he might well have said: "Get her for me, for I must be about my Father's (for God is the one who really birthed him) business." The overall intent of both statements (made by Jesus and Samson) appears very much the same—that is, to follow the divine purpose for which they were born into the world.

It is very significant to note that in both scenarios neither set of the parents knew or understood what providence was doing in the experience of their children. Judges 14:4 says of Samson's parents: *"His father and mother did not know that this was from the LORD; for he was seeking a pretext to act against the Philistines. At that time the Philistines had dominion over Israel.* In similar fashion, Luke 2:50 says of Mary and Joseph: *"And they did not understand the statement which He had made to them."*

This is just simply amazing, and it underscores the

fact that sometimes it is exceedingly difficult (or even impossible) to explain to others, especially those who are close to us, what the Almighty is doing in our lives. Quite often, we ourselves do not, and cannot, fully comprehend the meaning of our life's journey—let alone explain that journey to others. God's "strange" methods always defy the natural, logical reasoning of man.

This brings us right back to the opening question of this section, and the main issue of this chapter. Was Samson determined to be a disobedient, rebellious son when he completely ignored the counsel of his parents and requested that they follow through with his demand for a wife from among the daughters of the Philistines? Certainly not! What may have appeared as disobedience in the eyes of his parents, and upheld by the court of popular Christian opinion, was, in truth and in fact, the shining model of fearless faith.

Interestingly, Samson's response to his protesting parents (*"Get her for me, for she looks good to me"*) also mirrored the repeated refrain in the experience of Israel with regard to their spiritual apostasy against God: *"every man did what was right in his own eyes"* (Judges 17:6; 21:25). It is a case of Samson mirroring in his flesh what the nation was doing in the spirit.

This son of Israel exemplified the life of a faithful servant, who was willing to go against the grain of the religious and cultural norms of his society, and his Nazirite upbringing, to mirror in his flesh the failings of a rebellious nation, and follow his high calling to be God's lightning rod for the destruction of the Philistines. This was a very lonely road, which only God (who called) and Samson (who obeyed) understood. Nonetheless, it was a very noble path, and Samson was determined to pursue it.

Samson and You

God's purposes always reign supreme. They are always directed and supported by His sovereign will that can, at times, override, but in no wise negates, any of His previous commands. This fact is often very difficult for the logical human mind to comprehend, and we are often bewildered when God appears to do something out of character with what He previously ordained.

For example, in the sixth commandment, God specifically prohibits the slaying of another human being; but in order to accomplish His purpose for His people Israel, He instructed them to kill, without mercy, the people of the heathen nations in their immediate surroundings, in the land of promise. Israel was commanded not to leave alive anything that breathed. See Deuteronomy 20:16-18; Joshua 11:11-15; Samuel 15:2, 3, 11. He, not us, alone determines what is lawful, or unlawful killing.

Similarly, how do we explain the fact that God raised up Pharaoh for the specific purpose of demonstrating His power in him so that His name would be proclaimed throughout the whole earth (Romans 9:17)—and it was (Exodus 23:27; Joshua 2:8-11; 9:9, 10, 24)?

Further, how could we reconcile God's instruction that the priests of Israel should not to be joined in marriage to a woman who had been profaned by harlotry (Leviticus 21:7, 14) with His command to His chosen prophet (Hosea, although not a priest) to marry a temple whore?

Like Samson, Hosea's marriage to Gomer was intended to serve God's purpose of graphically portraying Israel's adulterous affair with the gods of the heathen nations that surrounded them (Hosea 1:2; 3:1-3). In any event, such apparent contradictions can be very troubling, and may create a great deal of mental stress and confusion for the average believer; but these are the divine *X-files* that have troubled the sages and Christian apologists for centuries.

The apostle Paul tackles some of these theological Gordian knots (divine *X*-files) in his letter to the Romans, and courageously exalts and confirms God's sovereignty and divine prerogative. He wrote:

> For this is the word of promise: "AT THIS TIME I WILL COME, AND SARAH SHALL HAVE A SON." [10]And not only this, but there was Rebekah also, when she had conceived twins by one man, our father Isaac; [11]for though the twins were not yet born and had not done anything good or bad, <u>so that God's purpose according to His choice would stand</u>, <u>not because of works but because of Him who calls</u>, [12]it was said to her, "THE OLDER WILL SERVE THE YOUNGER."

¹³Just as it is written, "JACOB I LOVED, BUT ESAU I HATED."

¹⁴What shall we say then? There is no injustice with God, is there? May it never be! ¹⁵For He says to Moses, "<u>I WILL HAVE MERCY ON WHOM I HAVE MERCY, AND I WILL HAVE COMPASSION ON WHOM I HAVE COMPASSION.</u>" ¹⁶So then <u>it does not depend on the man who wills or the man who runs, but on God who has mercy.</u>

¹⁷For the Scripture says to Pharaoh, "<u>FOR THIS VERY PURPOSE I RAISED YOU UP, TO DEMONSTRATE MY POWER IN YOU, AND THAT MY NAME MIGHT BE PROCLAIMED THROUGHOUT THE WHOLE EARTH.</u>"

Romans 9:9-17

These are very hard sayings for the limited parameters of our human mind; but faith in God Almighty does not, and cannot put terrestrial reins on the scope of divine providence. It is very difficult for mortal man to understand or accept the fact that not everything that God does is subject to our intellectual discussion, higher investigation, theological dissecting, or empirical evaluation.

In the above passage, Paul explains that God made the choice of Jacob over Esau, not only because His divine prerogative gave Him every right to do so; but in order that His purpose with regard to the birthright and its blessing would stand on His mercy and grace and not on the works of human logic and tradition.

It was both traditional and logical for Esau, not Jacob, to be the recipient of the birthright (as is customary with so many other man-made accolades and awards), but by His merciful kindness, God bestowed the precious gift to Jacob. How mind-boggling are the ways of God to the ways of man. In the end there is absolutely no room for human boasting. Paul explains this very idea in 1 Corinthians 1:27-29:

> ... but God has chosen the foolish things of the world to shame the wise, and God has chosen the <u>weak things</u> of the world to shame the things which are strong, ^{28}and the <u>base things</u> of the world and <u>the despised</u> God has chosen, the <u>things that are not</u>, so that He may nullify the things that are, ^{29}<u>so that no man may boast before God</u>.
>
> 1 Corinthians 1:27-29

In God's dealing with Pharaoh, it is also quite evident that divine purpose always takes precedence over human existence. This was also true for John the Baptist and Samson. As soon as their missions were over, the reason for their existence became obsolete. As was stated above, God made the unilateral choice (and who can contest Him or resist His will? – Romans 9:19) to bring Pharaoh into the world to demonstrate His awesome power to the Egyptian dynasty, and all the nations in the land of promise beyond the Jordan.

It was, and is, the same God who designed (or raised) one vessel (individual) for honor, and the other for dishonor. This is a very difficult issue for our finite intelligence to perceive or even accept; but there are some things that God decrees for His eternal purpose that no amount of human query can justify or explain.

We simply do not possess the mental capacity to fathom the Almighty to perfection (Job 11:7), because we do not know all the truth which pertains to God's omnipotent actions. Therefore, as mortal men, we must tread very carefully, and quite often "ponder anew what the Almighty can do . . ."[1] Paul continues his affirmation of God's sovereign rule and authority:

> *You will say to me then, "Why does He still find fault? For who [could] resist His will?"* [20]*On the contrary, who are you, O man, who answers back to God? The thing molded will not say to the molder, "Why did you make me like this," will it?* [21]*Or does not the potter have a right over the clay, to make from the same lump one vessel for honorable use and another for common use?*

> *²²What if God, although willing to demonstrate His wrath and to make His power known, endured with much patience vessels of wrath prepared for destruction? ²³And He did so to make known the riches of His glory upon vessels of mercy, which He prepared beforehand for glory, ²⁴even us, whom He also called, not from among Jews only, but also from among Gentiles.*
>
> Romans 9:19-24

It is very obvious from the passages of scripture cited above that God does not need any human being, however brilliant, to defend His decisions or His actions. God (the divine Potter) makes absolutely no apologies for what He does with His clay. He takes full and complete responsibility for all that He commands, all which He ordains, and all that He performs. He will have mercy and compassion upon whom He wills, according to His purpose, so that His choice in any matter will stand.

God's decisions are not influenced by man's opinions or self-righteous works, but by His purpose and His mercy. God is God all by Himself, and does not require any religious apologists or well-meaning individuals to defend Him by offering reasons or justifications for what they do not really understand. God is the justifier of all who believe in Him (Romans 3:26). May we never forget!

Quite often we come to the Bible with these very

limited, fixed images of God in our minds; and then we stumble upon such passages like Romans 9:9-24, God's curse on king Saul (1 Samuel 16:14, 15; 18:10; 19:9), or even our current Samson saga, and we are totally baffled. Such incidence tends to fill us with unwarranted fear—not really for God and what others may think about Him, but for ourselves and how we will relate to our discovery.

God will always be God, whether we choose to believe or not to believe what is written, as it is written. It is the weakness of our faith (or lack thereof) to grasp His limitless vastness and incontestable sovereignty, and not God's holy, righteous character that becomes suspicious and questionable. Our heavenly Father is faithful, always.

Our conceptions of the great God of the universe are often too small. We have the human tendency to confine the Almighty and His actions to the limits of our logical reasoning. We often forget that God is the One who has established His throne in the heavens and that His sovereignty rules over everyone and everything in His expansive universe (Psalm 103:19).

How much longer will we continue to try to place God within our constricted, human logic-boxes, and He then has to step outside our "secure," minuscule containers to display His awesome power and sovereignty, leaving us totally flabbergasted? Let God be God! Flesh will always be flesh; but let your faith learn to embrace the Almighty for who He is. If you were able to weigh God's motives and understand all His ways, then He would no longer be whom you claim Him to be; for you would then become greater than He.

Remember, Samson believed God, and God, Samson's *X-Factor*, did great things through him in spite of his humanity. You can do the same and expect similar results. Only, let God be God, and leave all the details of the what, when, where, how and why up to Him.

Notes:

1. Line taken from Joachim Neander's hymn, *Praise to the Lord*, in The Church Hymnal (Washington D.C.: Review and Herald Publishing Association, 1941), 18.

SAMSON X-FILE

MY THOUGHTS

DISOBEDIENT SON OR FEARLESS SERVANT?

3

UNDER THE INFLUENCE

Then Samson went down with his father and mother to Timnah. When he came to the vineyards of Timnah, suddenly a young lion roared at him. ⁶<u>*The spirit of the LORD rushed on him*</u>*, and he tore the lion apart barehanded as one might tear apart a kid.* <u>*But he did not tell his father or his mother what he had done*</u>*.*

⁷Then he went down and talked with the woman, and she pleased Samson. ⁸After a while he returned to marry her, and he turned aside to see the carcass of the lion, and there was a swarm of bees in the body of the lion, and honey.

⁹He scraped it out into his hands, and went on, eating as he went. When he came to his father and mother, he gave some to them, and they ate it. <u>*But he did not tell them that*</u>

> *he had taken the honey from the carcass of the lion.*
>
> Judges 14:5-9, NRSV

Rush Power I – Dealing With Your Lion

Although Samson's parents were not in agreement with his choice for a wife, they chose to comply with his request and began making preparations to arrange the marriage. It was customary in those times for parents to orchestrate marriages between their children, and for the parents of the prospective groom to initiate the marital contract with the parents of the bride-to-be. Accordingly, Samson's parents accompanied him on perhaps his second visit to Timnah in order to carry out such an arrangement.

It would appear that while Manoah and his wife were busily engaged in drawing up the marriage contract with the parents of their son's would-be bride, Samson was out walking through the vineyards of that country. It was during that exploratory tour that a young lion suddenly appeared out of the bushes and threateningly charged at Samson. Instantaneously, the Spirit of the Lord rushed mightily upon him and Samson barehandedly tore the lion to pieces as one would a worn-out garment.

Whether this attack by the young lion was a symbolic representation of what Samson was going up against in his relationship with the Philistines, the story does not say; but one is left to wonder. However, the fact is that God was willing and ready to match any challenge that His chosen vessel would face while pursuing his divine assignment. It is very interesting to observe that just as suddenly as the young lion attacked Samson, the Spirit of God rushed upon him to take care of the fatal emergency.

    Samson's victory over the young lion was a very crucial endorsement of what God was going to do to the Philistines at the hands of His servant. It represented, what I call, just-in-time power delivery. God is never late, but always on time—not according to our mind-clocks, but His providential purpose—working in unexpected situations, through unexpected means to mysteriously deliver and bless His children. Hymn-writer, William Poole, captured this fact so well when he wrote:

> Just when I need Him, Jesus is near
> Just when I falter, just when I fear;
> Ready to help me, ready to cheer,
> Just when I need Him most.

Refrain

> Just when I need Him most,
> Just when I need Him most;
> Jesus is near to comfort and cheer,
> Just when I need Him most.

> Just when I need Him, He is my all
> Answering when upon Him I call;
> Tenderly watching lest I should fall,
> Just when I need Him most.[1]

God delivered power and victory to Samson just when he needed it, for He was operating under the influence of His Spirit. His complete demolition of this ravenous beast was a most impressive victory by any standard, yet he never mentioned this exploit to anyone, not even his parents. To me, this crucial omission is very significant, and clearly suggests that both Manoah and his wife were not ready to deal with the *X-file* that God was opening on their son's life. Thus, Samson deliberately withheld information from his parents regarding his victorious encounter with the young lion (Judges 14:6).

Shortly thereafter, Samson socialized with his intended bride and her parents, but never revealed the exciting event that had only recently happened in his life. When the ceremonial contract was completely arranged, Samson returned home with his parents, but stored the treasure of God's dealing with him in his heart. This consecrated warrior simply chose to conceal what the Lord was doing in and through him. By doing so, Samson made certain that no one would be given the opportunity to misappropriate the glory that belonged to God, or attempt to misrepresent the working of God's power in his life.

Sweet Reward

When Samson returned to Timnah to take the hand of his beloved in marriage, the memory of his recent battle caused him to turn aside to look again upon the trophy of his victory. What he saw surprised him. Nestled in the cavity of the dead lion were a swarm of bees and a comb with dripping honey. Not intimidated by the buzzing hoard, he reached into the lion's carcass, retrieved a soggy lump of honeycomb, and began eating as he went along his way. As a dutiful son, he allowed his parents to share in the sweetness of his victory, but, again, he did not tell them from what source the honey came.

The fact that the author of the book of Judges took the time to draw our attention to Samson's "don't-tell" policy toward his parents the second time around (Judges 14:6, 9), is a clear indication that Samson was being very guarded about his life's mission (God's purpose). However, while neither Samson's parents nor the people of Israel knew or understood the contents of Samson's *X-file*, they were all going to share in the sweet reward that would be the result of his lonely, selfless sacrifice. How remarkably close this mirrors the experience of our Savior.

Samson and You

The story of Samson is a story of hope and triumph. It is a story that clearly portrays God's providence and faithfulness. Sometimes adversity may suddenly break out upon you as a young lion leaping out of a thicket, and chilling fear may sweep over your soul. In those times, remember that whatever (or whoever) those lion are, you have a God who can deliver just-in-time power for you to tear them to bits.

Do not be discouraged or dismayed; just give God the control over your situation and He will deliver you from your lion's paws. You must live daily under the divine influence, and God will be your *X-Factor*. He will turn the bitterness of your experience into the honey of sweet victory and rejoicing. Victory may be delayed, but it is certainly coming. Your weeping may endure for many nights, but your joy will break forth like the morning light.

Another very important lesson from this chapter is that, sometimes, you cannot make others privy to even the victories God is scoring in your life, because they may not understand them, and may not even be ready to read or receive the contents of your *X-file*. Moreover, not everyone will rejoice when you are victorious.

There are those who will be envious while pretending to be happy for you; there are others who will even be self-righteously critical in the face of your victory and blessing; and then there will be those who will completely misinterpret what your victory or blessing represents.

Nevertheless, do not allow anyone to restrain your joy and rejoicing when you desire to praise the Lord in the congregation of His people. At the same time, do not yield to the temptation to disclose what God is doing in your life before the time is right.

You will know when that time is, usually when the purifying, purging or perfecting process is over. Remember, the roaring lion (1 Peter 5:8) is always on the prowl, seeking to steal your dream through some human medium.

Notes:

1. William Poole, *Just When I Need Him*, in The Church Hymnal (Washington, D.C.: Review and Herald Publishing Association, 1941), 474.

MY THOUGHTS

SAMSON X-FILE

4

DANCING WITH FOXES

> *Then his father went down to the woman; and Samson made a feast there, for the young men customarily did this. When they saw him, they brought thirty companions to be with him.*
>
> Judges 14:10, 11

    The next significant event in the Samson saga was the occasion of his marriage to his Philistine sweetheart. To celebrate the great event and to give public recognition to His new status, Samson followed the traditional custom of throwing a large feast. These feasts usually lasted for a period of seven days, and consisted of numerous festivities, along with unrestrained eating and drinking. On this particular occasion, Samson had the unique privilege of having thirty young men in his personal attendance—the equivalent of our modern day groomsmen—ministering to his every need.

    Although Samson, himself, did not know these young men (they were obviously Philistines), he went along with the idea of partnering with them in conducting His wedding feast. Little did Samson realize that he was dancing with an unscrupulous pack of foxes that would set the stage for God (the *X-Factor*) to offer him his very first occasion to war against the Philistines.

Riddle, A-riddle, A-ree

In order to show his gratitude for the services of his Philistine groomsmen, along with trying to provide some additional entertainment for his guests, Samson assumed the role of a "riddler" and made a very ambitious proposal.

> Then Samson said to them, "Let me now propound a riddle to you; if you will indeed tell it to me within the seven days of the feast, and find it out, then I will give you thirty linen wraps and thirty changes of clothes. "But if you are unable to tell me, then you shall give me thirty linen wraps and thirty changes of clothes."
>
> Judges 14:12

After listening very quietly and carefully to Samson's deal, the young men eagerly replied: *"Propound your riddle, that we may hear it."* I could imagine a very broad smile coming over Samson's face as he prepares himself to declare his mystery statement. If he were living today, he might have said this: "*A-riddle, a-riddle, a-ree*, Out of the eater came something to eat, And out of the strong came something sweet (Judges 14:14). *It's the greatest mystery I've ever seen, can you tell me young men what does this riddle mean?*" [Italics, my addition]

For three days and nights the thirty young men racked their brains and consulted with one another concerning the answer to Samson's riddle, but they came up empty every time. Frustrated by their collective mental incompetence, and growing increasingly desperate because of their greed for gain, they decided to resort to coercive manipulation in order to achieve their end. These unscrupulous fellows targeted Samson's wife with a threatening demand.

Plowing with the Wrong Cow

> *Then it came about on the fourth day that they said to Samson's wife, "Entice your husband, so that he will tell us the riddle, or we will burn you and your father's house with fire. Have you invited us to impoverish us? Is this not so?"*

Judges 14:15

In her desperate attempt to save herself and her father's household from imminent destruction, Samson's wife began to use a woman's choice weapon of relational warfare (floods of tears), and reverse psychology, to pressure him into revealing to her the answer to his riddle. The Bible says that she wept before him and said, *"You only hate me, and you do not love me; you have propounded a riddle to the sons of my people, and have not told it to me"* (verse 16). Samson parries this heart-wrenching thrust with a resolute question: *"Behold, I have not told it to my father or mother; so should I tell you?"*

Samson's bride was now in an extremely difficult situation. She had already decided that nothing would get between her and her family, not even Samson. Now she was faced with the flip side of her own decision. How could she get between her husband and his parents? This was a bridal nightmare and still is today for those who are competing with their mothers-in-law for the respect and affection of their husbands.

When the stakes are high, it is quite inconceivable to imagine the lengths to which a spouse would go to achieve his or her purpose. During the seven days of the feast, which incidentally was also their honeymoon, Samson did not get any honey. His moon was drenched with crocodile tears. Samson's will was broken. What man could bear the tears of his red-eyed, honeymoon bride for seven straight days without yielding to her wishes? The story says that *on the seventh day he told her because she pressed him so hard. She then told the riddle to the sons of her people* (verse 17).

Gentlemen, be on guard, for sometimes the tears of a distraught woman possess mystifying power! The Italian proverb says that "women's tears are a fountain of craft." Some are quite capable of crying a river of tears in an instant (or for a week, if needs be) and then run off with your most treasured secret in a moment. Remember Samson!

The Philistine foxes had plowed their fields with the wrong cow (Samson's wife) and won. Thus, they came to Samson at the setting of the sun on the seventh day and declared the answer to his riddle: *"What is sweeter than honey? And what is stronger than a lion?"* And he said to them, *"If you had not plowed with my heifer, you would not have found out my riddle"* (verse 18). However, what these poor, crafty swindlers did not know was that behind the scene of their diabolical plan, the higher, unseen hands of Samson's *X-Factor* were setting up the occasion (Judges 14:4) for His servant to destroy their countrymen; and that Samson's loss was really God's gain.

Rush Power II – Outfitting the Groomsmen

Do not believe for one moment that Samson's actions were in isolation from God's overall purpose for his life. Far from it! This unfortunate marring of Samson's wedding was God's opportunity to initiate His campaign of destruction against the Philistines. Consequently, in order to meet the demands of Samson's proposal, the Spirit of the Lord rushed upon him and drove him down to Ashkelon to kill thirty Philistines. Samson then took his blood-washed spoil of probably mismatched, unfitting clothing and delivered them to his "foxy" groomsmen. One can only imagine their horror when they saw their ghastly reward.

Again, the Spirit of God empowered Samson the very moment he needed the supernatural assistance so that he could fulfill his divine assignment.

> Then the spirit of the LORD <u>rushed on him</u>, and he went down to Ashkelon. He killed thirty men of the town, took their spoil, and gave the festal garments to those who had explained the riddle. In hot anger he went back to his father's house.
>
> Judges 14:19, NIV

Samson and You

There may have been occasions in your lives when you have aligned yourselves with the wrong person or crowd (unknown to you at the time), with the hope of attaining some good for yourself or your family (whatever that good may be), only to have your life severely disrupted by the fallout from those relationships. Many of you have danced with some devious foxes in your lives, and when the party was over, you found yourselves utterly broken and lost. Then the merciful, unseen hand of the Almighty used your brokenness and depravity to demonstrate His power in your lives, and to display His providence as He drew you closer to Himself.

You may even be going through a really rough period right now because of some decision you have made in the past, but do not despair. Remember that God (the *X-Factor*) is standing in the shadows, keeping watch over His own. He is your right-on-time God—your present Help in times of every trouble (Psalm 46). He is able to use what may appear to you and others as a hopeless situation, to reveal His divine purpose in your life.

Therefore, look to Him and do not be afraid. Quite often, your apparent failures and disappointments turn out to be God's appointed agencies to clear your cloudy vision (colored by your faulty opinions, ideas and prejudices) about yourself and others, so that you could have an un-obstructive view of Him, and a loftier understanding of His perfect will and purpose for your life.

In the end, if you place your trust and confidence in God Almighty, He will take all the situations in your vapor-like existence, no matter how hopeless and irretrievable they may appear, and work them all out for your good, because you love Him. His purpose concerning you will most certainly stand, for *God causes all things to work together for good to those who love God, to those who are called according to His purpose* (Romans 8:28).

You must, therefore, stand solidly on His infallible Word. Set the sail of your faith God-ward and when the storms of life blow against your vessel (and they will), they will drive you closer to your Refuge and Shelter—the Master of earth, and sea, and sky. Just as God Almighty used the negative situation in Samson's life to fulfill His declared purpose concerning His servant, He can and will do the same for you and for me. Bless His holy name!

SAMSON X-FILE

MY THOUGHTS

5

FOR GOD, WIFE, AND COUNTRY

But after a while, in the time of wheat harvest, Samson visited his wife with a young goat, and said, "I will go in to my wife in her room." ²But her father did not let him enter. Her father said, "I really thought that you hated her intensely; so I gave her to your companion. Is not her younger sister more beautiful than she? Please let her be yours instead." ³Samson then said to them, "This time I shall be blameless in regard to the Philistines when I do them harm."

Judges 15:1-3

Forbidden Desire

It is woefully easy to read through every episode of the Samson saga and miss the very real human experience of isolation and loneliness that characterized this warrior's life. This is generally possible because we are so easily distracted by our pre-conditioned judgment of Samson's character and our absorption in the drama surrounding his every step. However, Samson was very much alone in his experience because no one, but the God who formed and called him, really understood the true purpose and meaning of his brief earthly existence.

While Samson knew he was called by God for the Philistine mission, and had yielded himself in obedience to that calling, he did not know what the events surrounding his life were going to be, or how they were going to unfold. Nevertheless, the God whom he served was always there for him when he needed Him.

Imagine this great God-warrior returning to his father's house after his wedding, without his wife and his bounty, but with a deep sense of betrayal and loss. He never had the opportunity to enjoy his honeymoon, or even the favor to consummate his marriage, because his tormented bride was not in the mood for love.

Samson's desire for love and affection was forcefully denied because of the threat of impending doom that was hanging over the head of his bride. To complicate the situation even further, Samson had to pay his manipulative, foxy companions for squeezing the answer for his riddle out of his wife. Although Samson made good on his promise to pay his deceitful comrades, he left the scene of his wedding a very hurt and angry man (Judges 14:19).

How long did it take for Samson to retrace his lonely steps to Timnah, the author of the book of Judges does not say. However, when he returned he entered the town carrying a peace offering to make things right with his wife. When he got to her father's house, he was denied access to her room. Her father said to him: *"I really thought that you hated her intensely; so I gave her to your companion. Is not her younger sister more beautiful than she? Please let her be yours instead"* (Judges 15:2).

What a disaster! I imagine that Samson was caught completely off-guard. Much to his utter distress, his wife had become a forbidden desire because one of the conniving foxes, who pretended to be his friend, was now her husband. Although his father-in-law tried to wiggle himself out of the very embarrassing quagmire by offering Samson the comparable substitute of his beautiful younger daughter, Samson was not willing to play switch-a-rue with the Philistines. There was absolutely no confirmation in Samson's spirit for his wife's sister.

Foxy Fire

> *³Samson then said to them, "This time I shall be blameless in regard to the Philistines when I do them harm." ⁴Samson went and caught three hundred foxes, and took torches, and turned the foxes tail to tail and put one torch in the middle between two tails. ⁵When he had set fire to the torches, he*

> *released the foxes into the standing grain of the Philistines, thus burning up both the shocks and the standing grain, along with the vineyards and groves.*

> Judges 15:3-5

One can only imagine all the thoughts that instantly flooded Samson's mind after his father-in-law completed his conciliatory speech. "These Philistines have cheated me out of my reward for their ignorance regarding the answer to my riddle; they forcefully exploited my wife and cheated me out of my honeymoon happiness; now they have plotted and have taken the wife of my dreams altogether. Enough is enough!"

The divine warrior was livid. *"This time I shall be blameless in regard to the Philistines when I do them harm"* (Judges 15:3). What happened next is beyond human understanding and explanation. Like the sly foxes his companions were, Samson went out and caught three hundred of the very creatures (foxes), tied them tail to tail, with a torch within the knot that held the tails together.

How could one man have caught three hundred wild foxes all by himself? This, by far, surpasses human understanding. How could he have single-handedly tied these sly, ravenous creatures tail to tail? I could only surmise that Samson had behind-the-scenes supernatural help (the *X-Factor*). Undoubtedly, his actions were in proper alignment with the divine operative to destroy the

Philistines (Judges 14:4).

The Bible says that when he had set fire to the torches, tied between the tails of each pair of foxes, he released the petrified animals in the fields of the Philistines, completely destroying the stocks and the standing grain, along with the vineyards and the groves (Judges 15:5). That foxy fire had proven to be a most disastrous conflagration, wreaking havoc on the Philistine's frail economy and disrupting their worship system—for those who worshipped their gods in the groves.

Flaming Escalation

Samson's actions ignited the ire of the Philistines, but instead of dealing directly with him, they believed it would hurt him more if they carried out the threat they had made against his wife and her father's household. Is it not ironic that the very disaster Samson's wife tried to avert by revealing to the Philistines the answer to her husband's riddle, is the very judgment that came upon her entire family? The Philistines came and executed their flaming revenge by torching her and her father.

What a strange escalation of events. It is rather interesting to observe that after Samson learned that his wife was given to another man, he did not direct his anger and frustration toward his immediate family of in-laws. Instead, he targeted the whole Philistine community (Judges 15:3). In the same manner, the Philistines retaliated, not by going after Samson who was responsible for the utter destruction of their livelihood, but by horribly burning his wife and her father.

I believe that this unnecessary escalation of events was providentially orchestrated, and paved the way for God to carry out His plan to use Samson to destroy the Philistines. Hence, the brief cordial relationship between Samson and the Philistines had become a thing of the past; and with the death of his wife, the stage was permanently set for open war and untold destruction.

Consequently, Samson vowed: *"I will surely take revenge on you, but after that I will quit"* (Judges 15:7). Yeah right! (colloquially speaking). At least, that was what Samson intended to do; but he had completely failed to remember that he was not the one making all the decision in his life, as he certainly found out later. He simply did not take into account the fact that he was not only fighting for himself and his wife, but also for God and his country. In the ruthless rampage that followed, Samson mercilessly slaughtered an untold number of Philistines, after which he retired to live in a mountain cave in a place called Etam.

Samson and You

In this episode of Samson's life, it would appear that the intense build-up of the conflict between this great warrior and the Philistines was unavoidable owing to the providential outworking of God's divine purpose. However, in normal life situations one would do well to avoid unnecessary escalation in a conflict situation in order to enjoy and maintain one's peace of mind. One sure way to reduce the occurrence of such escalation is to restrict the resolution of the conflict situation to the people directly involved, and resist the powerful temptation to draw others into it.

Of course, Samson and the Philistines did otherwise, hence the disastrous results of their decisions. Seek peace and pursue it (Psalm 34:13) wherever possible, for the spirit of revenge is the destroyer of personal peace and the prison house from which the soul is never set free. Remember, forgiveness is not only meant to release the one who is indebted to you, or the one who has wronged you; forgiveness is meant to set you free from the poison of a hateful spirit. May the God of peace grant you His wisdom and grace to de-escalate all the conflict situations in your life, so that you may experience His perfect peace.

MY THOUGHTS

SAMSON X-FILE

6

GOD'S ARMY OF ONE

Then the Philistines went up and camped in Judah, and spread out in Lehi. The men of Judah said, "Why have you come up against us?" And they said, "We have come up to bind Samson in order to do to him as he did to us."

Judges 15:9, 10

Samson's crushing defeat of the Philistines precipitated a national crisis and an all-out vendetta against the Hebrew champion. The frustrated Philistines sent their armies to camp against the city of Judah, to hold it as ransom in exchange for their native son—Samson. When the leaders of Judah saw the armies of the Philistines they were greatly perplexed and very much afraid. *"Why have you come up against us?"* they inquired. In answer to the inquiry, the Philistines declared their very ambitious objective: *"We have come up to bind Samson in order to do to him as he did to us*" (Judges 15:10). The deadly game of tit-for-tat had escalated to national proportions and the Philistines were exacting the highest price—the lives of the people of Judah or its bound champion.

Binding the Strongman

The leaders of Judah were placed in dire straits. The Philistines were their masters, but Samson was their champion and bright hope for deliverance. How were they to deliver up their champion to the uncircumcised Philistines? Who among them would be able to bind the strong man? As the men of Judah assessed their situation, they decided to save themselves and struck a deal with the Philistines to bind Samson and deliver him into their hands. Accordingly, they sent a delegation (really an army) of 3,000 men to meet with Samson in his Etam stronghold, in order to resolve their very difficult situation.

The men of Judah opened their negotiations with Samson by posing two questions that reflected their position regarding the heightened conflict between the uncircumcised Philistines and their champion. *"Do you not know that the Philistines are rulers over us? What then is this that you have done to us"* (Judges 15:11)? Completely blinded by their own fears and woefully ignorant of God's dealings with his servant, they pointed the finger at Samson. Their questions revealed that they had resigned themselves to the dominion of the Philistines because they had lost their faith in the Lord of all the earth. Although the sons of Judah were not linked to the Philistines by marriage, they endeavored to appease the gods and leaders of the Philistines by yielding to their demands.

However, Samson would not accept their accusation because he was not afraid of the Philistines and would not be ruled by them. *"As they have done to me, so I have done to them,"* was his reply. What this Jewish commission and the Philistines did not know was that Samson was not totally responsible for all the disaster that had transpired throughout the country. They had absolutely no idea that Samson was a one-man army, although he was not physically and anatomically different from any other man. However, he had a secret source of power, an *X-Factor*, who was greater than any army and bigger than any man that ever lived.

Mistaken Assessment

The men of Judah went on to state their real purpose for interrogating Samson, hoping that their sheer numbers would be enough to convince him to comply with their request. *"We have come down to bind you so that we may give you into the hands of the Philistines"* (Judges 15:12). Samson agreed to be bound, not because he was intimidated by the 3,000-strong delegation from Judah, but because it was in the will of God and, therefore, his best interest that he did so. Samson knew that he could not attack the men of Judah because they were not the specified target of his divine assignment.

God did not raise and appoint him to destroy the tribe Judah, or the people of Israel, for that matter; Samson was a consecrated vessel for the destruction of the Philistines (14:4). Consequently, he struck a deal with the men of Judah and made them covenant with him regarding his life. *"Swear to me,"* he said, *"that you will not kill me"* (15:12). The men of Judah assured him that all that they were prepared to do was to bind him and turn him over to the Philistines; but that they would not put forth their hand to kill him.

It is quite ironic that the men of Judah were seeking to bind the one who was appointed by God to set them free. The spiritually and physically bound were seeking to bind the one who was really free. This reminds me of another Servant of God who was bound by the leaders of His own people and turned over to the Gentiles (Romans) to execute judgment against Him. He too was appointed by God to set His blinded captors and a world of sinners free.

Jesus allowed Himself to be bound, just as Samson did, knowing that he could have called a legion of angels to quickly deliver Him from the hands of the miserable delegation sent to apprehend him. Christ's captors, like the Hebrew commission sent to arrest Samson, probably escorted the Messiah away with the mistaken idea that they were responsible for His apprehension, but their grossly incorrect assessment was soon to be made manifest. For Christ it came at His glorious resurrection; for Samson, only moments after his arrest.

Rush Power III – Jawbone Justice

Samson was quite aware of the fact that, apart from his *X-Factor*, he was powerless over Judah and all Israel. However, once he was delivered into the hands of the Philistines, he knew he would be released from the covenant that bound him to the men of Judah, and would be free to open God's floodgate of fury on His enemies. Therefore, Samson allowed himself to be escorted from his rocky hideout, bound by two new ropes, under guard, and in the company of 3,000 men. What a remarkable spectacle that must have been, possibly drawing the attention of everyone in the local community.

If this were today, every news camera in town would have been there, vying for its share of the excitement. I could imagine people whooping and hollering at the top of their lungs, "Samson is taken!" "The strong man is captured!" As a matter of fact, the Bible says that as soon as the escort party got to Lehi and the Philistines saw Samson, they all started shouting as they advanced to meet him (Judges 15:14). In that very instant everything began to change, while eyes and mouths remained wide open.

> . . . and <u>the Spirit of the LORD rushed on him</u>, and the ropes that were on his arms became like flax that has caught fire, and his bonds melted off his hands. Then <u>he found a fresh jawbone of a donkey</u>, reached down

and took it, and with it he killed a thousand men.

Judges 15:14, 15, NRSV

Picture the mass hysteria as the Spirit of God, working through God's army of one, began the explosive slaughtering of the Philistines. This was the eminent display of God's just-in-time power for the just-in-time moment. Everyone who came to witness the demise of the Hebrew champion saw an awesome display of the power of Samson's God. First the ropes—they snapped as a piece of thread caught in a fire; then a fresh jawbone of a donkey—swinging left and right, up and down, as it mowed down the ranks and files of the advancing victims.

The Bible simply says he found it; but I do not believe that that jawbone just happened to be there, just at the right time for Samson to make use of it. I am strongly tempted to believe that *X-Factor* provided that unusual weapon of warfare to execute justice against the Philistines. When Samson was through, a thousand men lay scattered all around him, as crowds scampered in horror over the bloody devastation. I could only wonder what the Jewish escort party was saying about the effectiveness of their "overpowering" seizure.

Victory Song

Like the lion he was, the victorious champion

began to roar, waving his jawbone in the air as he shouted his triumphant song: *"With the jawbone of a donkey, heaps upon heaps, with the jawbone of a donkey I have slain a thousand men"* (Judges 15:16). At the end of his very short chant, Samson threw away the donkey's jawbone and called the place Ramath-lehi, or the high place of the jawbone.

Confirmed Favor

The very first record of Samson ever speaking to God in the entire four chapters of the book that portrays his life is found immediately following his slaughter of the Philistines. By the time Samson was through decimating the enemy, he was extremely exhausted and very thirsty, even to the point of death. In his anguish to quench his dire thirst, he cried out to the Lord, his God, and his very short prayer revealed that Samson clearly understood his relationship to his divine Commissioner and Commander.

The first words out of his mouth expressed gratitude and thanksgiving to God for the great deliverance He had wrought through him (Samson), testifying to the fact that Samson was not in doubt as to who was responsible for all his victories. He knew that the battles he was called to fight were not his, but the Lord's. Thus, he gave honor to whom honor was rightly due.

With what little strength he had left, the very tired warrior pressed a petition to his God in the form of a rhetorical question: *"How shall I die of thirst and fall into the hands of the uncircumcised*" (Judges 15:18)? In other words, "my God, how can you give me such a glorious victory over these uncircumcised Philistines and then let me fall into their hands because I am dying of thirst?

God immediately answered His servant, not with words, but with relevant action. He split open the little valley in Lehi, as He did before Moses and Israel in the wilderness of Sin (Exodus 17:6), and water gushed out to satisfy Samson's ravenous thirst. Immediately, the warrior's strength was renewed and his spirit was revived within him. By this simple miraculous act of grace and good favor, God confirmed Samson's victory over his enemies.

Samson and You

Sometimes compliance can be mistaken for weakness by those who are out of touch with the Source behind your calm and quiet confidence—that is, your *X-Factor*. This was certainly true in Samson's case, and will also prove true in some of the situations you will encounter in your life. However, meekness is not a sign of weakness, but it is the undeniable evidence that divine reins have a firm grip on all the God-given endowments that characterize your humanity. In meekness there is the uncommon ability to have the strength of a Lion, yet manifest it through the grace of a sacrificial Lamb; or to possess the explosive power of a champion like Samson and yet receive guidance at the hand of a child (Judges 16:26).

Meek compliance does not have to be the product of fear, but could represent a quiet strength and resolute confidence in what God can do through you. In His inaugural kingdom address, Christ clearly indicated that there is a special blessedness that resides in the individuals who are possessed by this heavenly trait; for God delights to manifest His perfect strength through our weakness—really meekness (2 Corinthians 12:9).

Through Samson's experience, it is also helpful to remember that you do not have to fight the battles of life all by yourself, using the weapon of the flesh—irrespective of how strong, sophisticated and adequate these may appear to be. God is ever willing and ready to fight for you, but you must surrender the battles to Him. This is the hard part, because we tend to allow our human logic to eclipse or even destroy our faith in Jehovah.

Through Samson's experience, it is also helpful to remember that you do not have to fight the battles of life all by yourself, using the weapon of the flesh—irrespective of how strong, sophisticated and adequate these may appear to be. God is ever willing and ready to fight for you, but you must surrender the battles to Him. This is the hard part, because we tend to allow our human logic to eclipse or even destroy our faith in Jehovah. Consequently, we ask God for help, but we refuse to turn the fight over to Him. We keep our focus on the *things seen*—that is, our situation and our problems—instead of on the *things not seen*—that is, God and His promises (2 Corinthians 4:18), not fully understanding that the divine *X-Factor* in our lives uses the *things which are not* to cancel or bring to naught the *things which are* (1 Corinthians 1:28).

Samson obviously knew the power which stood behind him and operated within him, so he was willing to surrender himself and his battles to God. You must learn to do the same, but in order to do that you must spend the time getting to know the God of Samson. You must plug into the Source of Samson's power—studying and meditating upon His Word, dialoguing with God through prayer, and fellowshipping with like-minded power-seekers. Remember that Samson was like any other man, except for the power of God that flowed through him.

Finally, be aware that God's way of fighting warfare is not the same as your way. He reminds you, through His servant Isaiah that His thoughts are not your thoughts, nor are your ways His ways, for *as* the heavens are higher than the earth, so are His ways higher than your ways and His thoughts than your thoughts (Isaiah 55:8, 9).

Thus, when you surrender the battle to Him, He may call you to use some strange weapons of warfare that will often challenge you, but will always confuse the enemy. For example, He may call you to love your enemy instead of hating him/her; to reach out instead of waiting to be approached; to give instead of expecting to receive; to seek peace instead of declaring war; to give in instead of fighting back; to praise instead of criticizing the enemy; and even to do nothing instead of trying to find something to do.

Jawbone justice is a vivid reminder that God is the one who chooses the instrument of war and not us. In the thick of your battle, you, like Samson, will suddenly find your "jawbone" that will effectively destroy the enemy. However, do not be surprised if you find that the weapon that you wield is not one of destruction, but one of instruction or even construction; for all of life's battles are not meant to destroy those you consider your enemies, but rather to bring salvation to them and, most of all, to yourself. In the light of all these facts, you will do well to remember and practice the words of the apostle Paul, who said:

> *For though we live in the world, <u>we do not wage war as the world does</u>. <u>The weapons we fight with are not the weapons of the world</u>. On the contrary, they have divine power to <u>demolish strongholds</u>. We <u>demolish arguments</u> and <u>every pretension</u> that sets itself up against the knowledge of God, and we take captive <u>every thought</u> to make it obedient to Christ.*
>
> 2 Corinthians 10:3-5

Above all, be always ready for your ultimate challenge, because the strongholds, arguments, pretension and thought you may be called upon to demolish may be your very own, since your greatest enemy is indeed yourself.

MY THOUGHTS

SAMSON X-FILE

7

PHILISTINE ADDICTION OR PUZZLING PROVIDENCE?

Now Samson went to Gaza and saw a harlot there, and went in to her.

Judges 16:1

A major challenge that confronts anyone reading the story of Samson is that the writer does not give any insight, or information regarding any dialogue between God and Samson, to help the reader to "logically" decipher the reason for Samson's repetitive encounters with Philistine women. One would think that after his very frustrating and short-lived relationship with his first wife, and the disastrous fallout of war and bloodshed that resulted, Samson would have turned to the daughters of his people and kept as far away as possible from the daughters of the Philistines.

However, the opposite was true; Samson never even considered a relationship with a daughter of Israel.

He merely distanced himself from the town of Timnah, headed for another city of the Philistines, Gaza. What was even more disconcerting was the fact that he went and joined himself to a prostitute of that city. Now what would have made this servant of God do something outlandish like that? How could a Nazirite, separated unto God, have lain with a city prostitute, without engendering the wrath of the Almighty?

Providence and Prostitutes

The answer to the questions above may possibly be found in the unnatural relationship between divine Providence and peddling prostitutes that is mirrored in several places throughout scripture. The very first prostitute with a providential agenda that we come across in the bible is the woman Rahab of Jericho. This voluptuous damsel lived on the wall of that great city, and her home became the house of choice for the spies sent by Joshua to scout out the land. It made perfect sense for these spies to target Rahab's house since she was used to having all types of men visit her home, therefore their presence there would not raise unnecessary suspicion.

Nevertheless, the word got out somehow, for the city of Jericho had spies of its own. The king of the city was informed of the presence and deadly mission of the sons of Israel holed up in Rahab's house, and he sent word that they should be brought to him. But Rahab feared the Lord; therefore she hid the men and fabricated a story about them exiting the city. Later that night, this harlot would testify to the spies:

> [9]*"I know that the LORD has given you the land, and that the terror of you has fallen on us, and that all the inhabitants of the land have melted away before you...* [11]*for the LORD your God, He is God in heaven above and on earth beneath.* [12]*Now therefore, please swear to me by the LORD, since I have dealt kindly with you, that you also will deal kindly with my father's household, and give me a pledge of truth, ...*
>
> Joshua 2:9, 11, 12

Notice the word of faith in the mouth of the prostitute: *"I know that the Lord has given you the land ... for the Lord your God, He is God in heaven above and on earth beneath."* What a confession of faith! Believe it or not, but this prostitute possessed more faith in the God of Israel than the ten spies (besides Caleb and Joshua) and the whole congregation they represented. Compare what Israel said about their God to Rahab's confession of faith.

> *"We are not able to go up against the people, for they are too strong for us."* [32]*So they gave out to the sons of Israel a bad report of the land which they had spied out, saying, "The land through which we have gone, in spying*

> *it out, is a land that devours its inhabitants; and all the people whom we saw in it are men of great size. ³³There also we saw the Nephilim (the sons of Anak are part of the Nephilim); and we became like grasshoppers in our own sight, and so we were in their sight . . ."*
>
> Numbers 13:31-33

> *²And all the sons of Israel grumbled against Moses and Aaron; and the whole congregation said to them, "Would that we had died in the land of Egypt! Or would that we had died in this wilderness! ³Why is the LORD bringing us into this land, to fall by the sword? Our wives and our little ones will become plunder; would it not be better for us to return to Egypt?" So they said to one another, ⁴"Let us appoint a leader and return to Egypt."*
>
> Numbers 14:2-4

Who among us is really qualified to judge another Man's servants (Romans 14:4)? Sometimes the sinners some professed Christians are prone to judge as hopelessly lost possess more faith in the God of heaven than the judges themselves. Paul's counsel is very instructive to all: *"Therefore let him who thinks he stands take heed that he does not fall"* (1 Corinthians 10:12).

It was because of her faith in God (limited as it may have been) and the favor she had shown His servants, that Rahab and her father's household were preserved when the children of Israel took the city of Jericho and completely destroyed it by fire. Furthermore, God extended greater honor to this "faithful" prostitute by not only making her a maternal grandparent of our Lord, Jesus Christ (Matthew 1:1, 5), but also by portraying her as an example of faith in the eleventh chapter of the book of Hebrews (verse 31).

Although God does not countenance or sanction the practice of prostitution, or the peddling of prostitutes, He clearly demonstrates that these victims of the evil one are not beyond the pales of His mercy and grace. We see Providence using Jephthah, the son of a prostitute, to be a mighty warrior and judge over His people Israel. The young man's half brothers drove him from his father's house because his mother was a prostitute, and they refused to share their father's inheritance with him.

However, the Almighty was looking out for Jephthah, for God (Jephthah's *X-Factor*) permitted a situation that required his gifted service, and the leaders of his city (Gilead) agreed to make him their judge (Judges 11:1-11). As this story reveals, God is not the one who really has the problem of dealing with prostitutes or the children of prostitutes. We do. And quite often we allow our prejudice toward prostitutes to color our understanding of God's dealings with them, pushing us to perform all sorts of mental gymnastics to fit God into our apologetic frameworks.

This is why the story of God's directives to the prophet Hosea baffles so many Christians, even scholars. How to interpret Hosea's marriage to Gomer is still a matter to be settled in many circles, because human reason cannot handle the sovereign, omnipotent God stepping outside its logic box to do what seem unthinkable—interacting with prostitutes.

Consequently, some "scholars" regard Hosea's marriage to Gomer as an allegory. Others think it was a literal marriage to a woman who became a prostitute after marriage. However, most "scholars" believe it is what the Word said it is—Hosea was directed to marry a cult (temple) prostitute for the specific purpose of being a living portrayal of Israel's unfaithfulness to God, and her adulterous affairs with the gods of the heathen nations. Here is another example of one of God's *X-files*.

What it is about Providence and prostitutes that is so intriguing? It is the simple fact that the sovereign God, who inhabits eternity, can take these victims of the enemy and make them show-pieces of His super-abounding grace and mercy; to declare His faithfulness in saving to the utmost anyone who comes to Him through the blood of His Son and our Savior, Jesus Christ.

Providence's gracious dealing with prostitutes, offers hope of salvation to all types of sinners—known and unknown. Hence, Jesus could have said of the prostitute, Mary Magdalene, who anointed His head and feet and was His faithful friend to the end—even when His most trusted disciples fled the scene at his arrest and crucifixion: *"Truly I say to you, wherever the gospel is preached in the whole world, what this woman has done will also be spoken of in memory of her"* (Mark 14:9).

Christ also gave this warning to the chief priests and leaders of Israel, and all those who think and behave like them: *"Truly I say to you that the tax collectors and prostitutes will get into the kingdom of God before you* (Matthew 21:31). Believe it or not; there is a safe place in the kingdom of God for all prostitutes, pimps and peddlers who come to faith in the Lord, Jesus Christ.

The Nazirite and the Prostitute

So what does Providence dealing with prostitutes have to do with Samson going in to a whore in the city of Gaza of the Philistines? Much in every way! We need to grasp the truth that the story of Samson is really less about him and more about his God. If we could only divert our attention from the distractions of Samson's life and focus on the revealed purpose of the mysterious *X-factor* that drove him, we would see that in his life, Samson was mirroring the spiritual experience of the tribe of Judah and all Israel.

The Samson story bears the truth about God's dealing with a backslidden bunch of slaves in a new land, and His sovereign purpose to deliver them through His chosen servants (Samson). In this great life drama, Samson reflected two very powerful images—namely, *rebellious sinner* and *suffering savior.* As the *rebellious sinner*,

Samson portrayed in the flesh what the children Israel lived in their relationship to God. As a *suffering savior*, Samson was ridiculed by his own people even though he was fighting against the Philistines for their safety and salvation.

Let's look at the facts of this story from the perspective of divine providence:

(1) Samson was separated unto God for the deliverance of Israel from the Philistines. Israel was also separated unto God, under Moses with the sprinkling of blood (Exodus 19:3-9; 24:8), to be a nation of priest unto God for the salvation of the world.

(2) Samson was joined to the Philistines in the flesh by marriage, but never in the spirit. On the other hand, the children of Israel were joined to the Philistines in the spirit (through the worship of their gods) although they did not give their sons and daughter in marriage to them in the flesh. Samson turned his back on the daughters of Israel so that he could be joined to a Philistine, just as Israel turned her back on her Lover (God) and was joined to the gods of the Philistines.

(3) Samson went in to a Philistine prostitute and lay with her all night until midnight; Israel was playing the harlot with the gods of the Philistines for many years (Judges 10:6), and this precipitated God's judgment on the nation. Thus, while Israel was looking aghast at what Samson was doing in the flesh, they were actually doing just like him,

and even more, with regard to their relationship with their spiritual Lover and Husband, Jehovah.

Now, how did God handle Samson's one-night stand with a prostitute? We must view every contact that Samson had with the Philistines through the scriptural lenses of the *X-file,* Judges 14:4—that is, God's occasion and opportunity to destroy them. The saga shows that while Samson was busily engaged with the harlot on the inside, his enemies were plotting his destruction and demise on the outside. They had bolted the main gate and sealed off every other exit from the city. Their plan was to ambush Samson at the crack of dawn and kill him. What these uncircumcised Philistines did not know was that Samson's *X-Factor* (Jehovah-Nissi) was watching over him and was poised to swiftly and effectively crush their plans. This was a divine set-up that was about to explode right in their faces.

The Bible says that Samson slept until midnight, not even till the crack of dawn, and then he awoke to leave. It is awfully strange what sometimes occur at midnight—the power goes out, the car breaks down, the storm hits, the earthquake rumbles, and evil things happen, even to good people. However, the cover of darkness and the glory of the light are both alike unto the divine Watcher, who often chooses to display His awesome power during the midnight hour.

It was at midnight that He sent great plagues upon Egypt and wrought the glorious deliverance of His people from cruel bondage. The Bible did not give the exact hour, but I believe that it was at midnight that an angel of the Lord opened the gates of the prison and released Peter and John and commanded them to stand before the people and teach them of the Lord, Jesus Christ (Acts 5:17-20).

I also believe that it was at midnight, that probably the same prison angel strode into the heavily guarded Roman dungeon, smote Peter on the side to wake him up. Then, along with Peter, the angel walked right back out of the prison—with chains falling off behind them and gates opening before them on their own accord (Acts 12:1-17). It was at midnight, while Paul and Silas were praising God, that He commissioned His prison angel to shake the foundation of the Roman prison to set His servants free. The shaking was so terrible that all the prison gates flew open and the jailer (and I believe other prisoners too) got saved that very night (Acts 16:22-34).

Rush Power IV – Storming the Gates of Hell

> *Now Samson lay until midnight, and at midnight he arose and took hold of the doors of the city gate and the two posts and pulled them up along with the bars; then he put them on his shoulders and carried them up to the top of the mountain which is opposite Hebron.*
>
> Judges 16:3

The account of what happened appears rather quite concise and somewhat matter-of-fact, or casual; but there is more here than meets the eye. Did Samson awake at midnight all on his own, or did the divine Watcher stir him up? I believe we can find the answer in what follows after this God-warrior awoke from his slumber. Samson did not just arise from his bed, take hold of the door of the city gate and root it out. Something had to have occurred between his leaving the house of the prostitute and his walk to the city gate. If we are to stay consistent with what happened to Samson whenever he encountered the Philistines, it is quite reasonable to believe that he had another rush of Holy Ghost power just before touching those gates. What Samson did to those gates and its pillars was not possible, by any stretch of the imagination, without some supernatural endowment.

Furthermore, whenever God wants to make a display of His majestic power, He does so with much fanfare so that no one would be left in doubt as to who was responsible for the awesome manifestation. Bursting through the door in the city gate would have been enough for Samson to make his escape, but that could have been easily misconstrued and been credited to the warrior's brute strength (which he really did not have apart from God). God wanted more, so He moved Samson to completely root up the gate, with its pillars and bars, from its foundation, put the entire contraption upon his shoulders, and carry it off to the top of the mountain opposite Hebron.

The Bible did not indicate how far the mountain was from the city. It well could have been a considerable distance. However, the mere idea that Samson took the gate with its pillars and climbed all the way up to the top of the mountain, while carrying the dismantled structure on his shoulders, was awesome enough to behold. What a terrifying display of strength and power this must have been to his on-looking "wanted-to-be captors". They must have stood completely mesmerized as they watched their "would-have-been" victim single-handedly prevail against the gates of their impending hell, and trek off with them on his shoulders as a shepherd would carry a wounded lamb of his flock.

If this were not the work of God, then what is? This incident represented the zenith of Samson's experience and career as God's warrior. This was his Rocky Balboa[1] moment, but only in reverse—since from that point on Samson set his face on the downward path toward Sorek and his eventual death. Samson could have simply rooted out the gate, cast it aside and gone on his way; but no! God wanted to make a statement by this warrior. No gate of hell, no matter how high or how wide, could prevail against the purpose and the power of the Almighty.

God was also telling the Philistines, through Samson, that He could liberate his people when He chose, and no wall or gate would be big or strong enough to prevent Him from doing so. Although Israel was living in spiritual midnight, shut in on all sides by the Philistines, while playing the harlot with their powerless gods, Jehovah was willing and ready to liberate her, if she would only awake from her iniquitous bed and come in faith to His victorious mountain.

Moreover, Samson's victory march to the mountain-top opposite Hebron, then down to Sorek and to his death, was a foreshadowing of Christ's victorious ascent to the mount of transfiguration, then down to Jerusalem and to His death. On top of the mount, Christ received words of comfort from Moses and Elijah prior to his death march to Jerusalem, and also heard His Father's approval, *"This is My beloved Son: hear Him"* (Luke 9:35). As the Master and His disciples left the scene of the mount, He began to teach and tell them: *"The Son of Man is to be delivered into the hands of men, and they will kill Him; and when He has been killed, He will rise three days later"* (Mark 9:31, KJV).

Flirting with Fire

> *After this it came about that he loved a woman in the valley of Sorek, whose name was Delilah. The lords of the Philistines came up to her and said to her, "Entice him, and see where his great strength lies and how we may overpower him that we may bind him to afflict him. Then we will each give you eleven hundred pieces of silver."*
>
> Judges 16:4, 5

Samson did it again. He went down into the valley of Sorek and fell in love with another Philistine woman called Delilah. Did this Nazirite servant of God have an addiction for Philistine women? Not necessarily, and no more than the children of Israel had an addiction for Philistine gods. However, Samson had a date with destiny which permanently linked him to the Philistines. It was for this very purpose that he was brought forth into the world.

When we combine what the angel of the Lord (Jesus Christ, Judges 13:20-22) said to Samson's mother (*and he shall begin to deliver Israel from the Philistines* – Judges 13:5), with God's purpose for having His servant seek a wife from the daughters of the heathen nation (*to seek an occasion to destroy them* – Judges 14:4), we see that Samson was indeed keeping a date with his destiny.

Thus, it was not by chance that this very lonely warrior fell for another heathen woman. Had it not been Delilah, it would have been some other Philistine damsel. However, from the very onset of this strange relationship, the lords of the Philistines sought to use Samson's love for Delilah as a form of leverage against him. After repeated dealings with the Hebrew champion, these leaders finally deduced that Samson's strength had to be coming from a source unknown to them—from some mysterious *X-Factor*.

In their estimation, there was no major visible evidence that gave Samson such significant advantages over them. Thus, they shifted their strategy from direct confrontation, which they realized they could not have won, to power neutralization, in order to level the battle field and improve their chances of victory. Delilah became their ultimate weapon, and they conspired with her to pry the secret out of her lover for the hefty price of eleven hundred pieces of silver.

Christ was sold out for thirty pieces of silver by a disciple that walked with Him for three years. The price on Samson's head was more than thirty-six times what was paid to Judas for him to betray his Master. This appeared to be an offer that Delilah was not prepared to refuse, not even for the love of the national champion. Thus, she employed all the finesse and charm at her disposal to seduce Samson into revealing the secret of his strength.

In the twenty years that Samson judged Israel, no one beside God and himself knew the real secret of his strength. Although there were many more Nazirites in Judah and Israel beside Samson, sporting uncut locks and unshaven beards, none of them possessed the explosive power of the son of Manoah. Samson had something more. He was divinely ordained by God through his miraculous birth to be God's output unit for demonstrating His power among the Philistines. His uncut locks were only an outward symbol of that unique covenant relationship with his Creator and Manager.

Although Samson cherished the secret of his relationship with God, the Source of his strength, and counted it a thing so precious to be concealed even from his parents, he flirted with the fire of love that he had in his heart for Delilah. It is very easy to take what you have received from God for granted when your heart is won over by a lover. On three occasions Samson danced with his destiny as he played spiritual Russian roulette with Delilah.

One would think that after the first and probably the second time around, it would have become clear to Samson what Delilah's intention was, and he would quit playing the game. Not Samson. He believed that he was safe as long as his secret remained hidden. However, what started out as fun and games began turning ugly, because Delilah was playing for keeps. Her time was running out and so were her chances on eleven hundred pieces of silver.

Crossing the Line

> [15]*Then she said to him, "How can you say, 'I love you,' when your heart is not with me? You have deceived me these three times and have not told me where your great strength is."* [16]*It came about when she pressed him daily with her words and urged him, that his soul was annoyed to death.* [17]<u>*So he told her all that was in his heart*</u> *and said to her, "A razor has never come on my head, for I have been a Nazirite to God from my mother's womb. If I am shaved, then my strength will leave me and* <u>*I will become weak and be like any other man.*</u>*"*
>
> Judges 16:15-17

Samson was obviously unprepared for what was coming upon Him. Although he had absolutely no intention of sharing the divine secret with Delilah, his flirtatious pandering had placed him in a very vulnerable position and set him up to do the unthinkable. When the nagging pressure of his pretentious lover was brought to bear upon the starving spirit of the lonesome warrior, he became emotionally unglued, and the divine secret he kept suppressed for more than twenty years, came pouring forth from his unrestrained lips. In the Caribbean islands there is a colloquial expression that describes this phenomenon, which says: *"mout'* (mouth) *open and 'tory* (story) *jump out!"* In other words, once Samson opened his mouth, every secret in his heart concerning himself came gushing out. The Bible says that he told her *all that was in his heart* (Judges 16:17).

What a tragedy! Samson had crossed the line and surrendered the secret of his strength for the love of a woman. The *X-file* was severely compromised and Samson exposed himself to grave danger. In revealing the secret of the *X-file*, the mighty champion allowed Delilah to share the space in his heart that was reserved for God alone. *"You shall have no other gods before me"* (Exodus 20:3). In that very moment, the Spirit, which consistently rushed upon him in time of need, in the same manner, instantly left him. The spark of power was gone without Samson knowing it (even before he fell asleep in Delilah's very rich lap), and the shaving of his head was only a symbol of the fact that the Spirit that once empowered Samson had already left.

Blinded and Bound; Not Defeated or Dead

The fearless warrior awoke from his slumber just as oblivious as when he fell asleep, not realizing that his complacent little cat-and-mouse game was over. *"He did not know that the Lord had departed from him"* (Judges 16:20). These were the saddest words of the entire Samson saga. When the champion attempted to shake himself free as he did the three times before, he came face to face with reality. His strength was completely gone and the Philistines were all over him, for he was then just *like any other man* (Judges 16:7, 11, 13, 16). The champion was absolutely devastated as he was humiliated by the rejoicing Philistines. They immediately plucked out his eyes, bound him with bronze chains, and took him away to grind grain in one of their prisons.

In this sad scenario of Samson and Delilah, we see another reflection of the relationship between the children of Israel and the gods of the Philistines. Samson dallied with Delilah just like Israel played the harlot by flirting in and out of her relationship with the Philistine' gods. The whole period of the Judges was a low point in Israel's history, marked by the repetitious behavior of apostasy and reconciliation, of dancing with the enemy and coming back to God.

Samson crossed the line then, just like Israel had and forfeited the presence of God's Spirit, leading the nation into a very chaotic period of history after the death of Samson. The writer of the book of Judges succinctly summed up the situation in the very last verse of the book. He said: *"In those days there was no king in Israel; everyone did what was right in his own eyes"* (Judges 21:25).

Ultimately, Israel remained in bondage under their Philistine masters, and continued so for a long time until the coming of her last judge, Samuel. However, in a very real sense, the blinding of Samson was a depiction of the spiritual blindness of Israel, and the binding of Israel's champion was also symbolic of Israel's bondage. Nevertheless, although Samson was blinded and bound, he was not completely defeated or dead, much to the ignorance and misfortune of his captors.

The Philistines thought that Samson's power was completely broken, that as long as they kept his head shaven, they would have him bound and battered (as they had Israel) until the day of his death. However, they were completely ignorant of the fact that Samson's strength was not in his hair, *but in his heart*; and that by keeping the notorious champion as a victory trophy to their god, and a spectacle of humiliation for their indulgent people, they were placing a ticking time-bomb in the bosom of their own community.

Putting Pieces Together

What we have just reviewed is a very amazing story of a valiant warrior, whose life is gravely misunderstood today as it was when he roamed his world. In Samson's brief relationship with Delilah we were actually looking at the mirror image of his love affair with his only wife, whose name was never given. She took his breath away very much like Delilah did; both women also betrayed Samson's trust for selfish reasons—one found death, the other, probably a rich life.

The truth is that the Samson experience follows a dynamic, chiasmatic[2] structure, with his mountain-top victory at Gaza standing at the center, and as the pinnacle of his life's journey; and on either side, the mirror images of the four defining events of his short, illustrious existence. These four events form the "mainframe" that ties together the major experiences of Samson's life:

A. We have the Mahaneh-dan experience, where Samson was stirred by the Spirit (Judges 13:25), which marked the launching of Samson's mission to initiate God's war against the Philistines.

B. The betrayal of Samson at Timnah (Judges 13:12-19) that actually set the stage for the predicted conflicts (Judges 14:4) that followed.

C. From the city of Timnah, there was a steady climb or building up of the conflict until Samson ascended his victory mountain opposite Hebron, after snatching the gates of Gaza (Judges 16:3).

B'. After the Gaza experience, Samson began trekking down the path to Sorek, and Delilah, where again he was betrayed into the hands of the Philistines (Judges 16:15-21).

A'. Finally, Samson is stirred at the end of his life, just as he was at its beginning, to engage the Philistines for the very last time (Judges 16:28-30)—closing the chapter on his very remarkable existence.

Following is an outline of this chiasm that summarizes the Samson saga:

> **A.** Samson stirred by the Spirit to engage the Philistines.
>
>> **B.** Samson's wife conspires with the Philistines to defeat him.
>>
>>> **C.** Samson snatches the gates of Gaza and treks to the mountain top opposite Hebron.
>>
>> **B'.** Delilah conspires with the Philistines to defeat Samson.
>
> **A'.** Samson stirred by the Spirit to destroy the Philistine at his death.

Please notice that **A** and **A'**, and **B** and **B'** are mirror images of each other; and **C** stands as the pinnacle and center of the structure. Below is a vertical representation of the same.

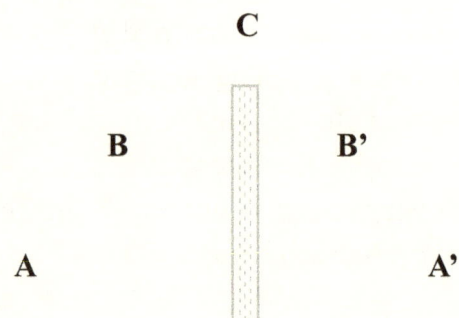

Samson and You

You must always keep in mind, as you read through this illustrative saga, that Samson was not your typical individual. His birth was strictly by God's appointment—his mother was barren—for a very specific purpose. Therefore, you must be aware that everything that is portrayed in Samson's life will not have a link or application to your personal experience. For example, sleeping with prostitutes (male or female) is not a righteous option for kingdom citizens even though God used such a situation in Samson's life to accomplish His purpose.

It may be very tempting for some to use the life of Samson as an excuse for their sinful pursuits. However, you should not place yourself under the influence and control of the enemy, and presume that the mercy of God will work out some miraculous deliverance for you. Sleeping with prostitutes is definitely not a Christian calling. It is a deadly curse (Hebrews 13:4; Revelation

21:8; 22:15). Danger awaits he/she who sleeps with the enemy!

Additionally, learn from Samson that when you think you are strong, that is the time you are most vulnerable. True strength comes, not from your ability to do or not do something, but rather from your choice to remain connected to the real Source of your strength. David correctly reminds us that *God is the strength of our [my] lives* Psalm 27:1. Samson's confidence in his strength (based on his past exploits), led him to trifle with Delilah and lose his hold on God. Beware my friend; for when you think you are strong, humiliation and destruction may be knocking at your door.

Godly wisdom will inform you that there is great strength in weakness, and also weakness in great strength. When the apostle Paul thought that having all his faculties intact and fully functioning would have made him a stronger Christian and a more powerful witness for Christ, the Savior had to correct his perspective by denying his thrice-repeated prayer request. When Christ finally answered, He gave Paul a message that is good for all of us today, and one which Samson did not remember: *"My grace is sufficient for you, for my power is made perfect in your weakness"* (2 Corinthians 12:9, NIV). This answer quickly changed Paul's concept about his weakness, and he most joyfully declared:

> *Most gladly, therefore, <u>I will rather boast about my weaknesses</u>, <u>so that the power of</u>*

> *Christ may dwell in me*. ¹⁰*Therefore I am well content with weaknesses, with insults, with distresses, with persecutions, with difficulties, for Christ's sake; for when I am weak, then I am strong.*
>
> 2 Corinthians 12:9, 10

God has all the power you need for every situation in your life. Make it your daily ambition and goal to stay plugged in to that power Source. Here is a wise counsel to always follow: *"Trust in the Lord with all your heart and lean not to your own understanding. In all your ways acknowledge Him and He will direct your paths"* (Proverbs 3:5, 6). Satan wants you to stay unplugged and depend on your own "wisdom" and "strength." Remember *"There is a way which seems right unto a man but its end is the way of death"* (Proverbs 16:25).

Sometimes the evil one will even use your sins and failings to depress you, to make you feel that you are not worthy enough to stay connected. Do not fall for this powerful downer! It is exactly at that time that your faith in the blood that already has been shed for your sins ought to rise above your fears and your failings, and tap into the empowering stream of the forgiveness and grace flowing from your power Source. Daily stay in the Word, continue in prayer and meditation, embrace the fellowship of the saints, engage in praise, and share the love of Jesus with others, no matter what happens.

When you are alone and there is no one to help or even listen to your cries, remember the Most High is the God of the midnight hour. He will comfort you, lift you up, deliver you, and wipe the tears from your eyes. He does not sleep or slumber (Psalm 121:3), but quietly awaits your audience with Him. In the midnight of your confusion and your dancing with iniquity and the enemy, when the evil one is plotting your demise and utter destruction, your compassionate Father will send you merciful, miraculous deliverance that will baffle your understanding. Such divine intervention will evoke from your trembling soul either songs of praise and rejoicing, or prayers of brokenness and repentance.

The Psalmist understood this very well and wrote: *"At midnight I shall rise to give thanks to Thee because of Thy righteous ordinances"* (Psalm 119:62). Paul and Silas took great advantage of the midnight hour to offer praise and thanksgiving to God and He shook the dungeon that imprisoned them. If things are going wrong in your world and you find yourself imprisoned by fear, doubt, complex problems, and adverse circumstances, just put on your pajamas or nightgown of praise during the midnight hour, and wait for the shaking of your prison house. It just might be that at midnight, while others are sound asleep, you may find that you have the presence of God all to yourself. He awaits your audience.

As an additional alert, please do not forget that if the enemy cannot conquer you through direct confrontation, he will use anyone and any situation to short circuit your connection to your power Source and completely neutralize you. Remember Samson!

Notes:

1. In the movie Rocky, the star character Rocky Balboa's (Sylvester Stallone's) speedy ascent to the pinnacle of a mountain or very tall building marked the turning point of his life from one of defeat to one of victory. For Samson, the opposite occurred, but with an ironic twist in the end—his death brought about the destruction of the Philistines and the freedom of his people.

2. A *chiasm* is a literary structure that depicts an inverted relationship between the syntactic elements of parallel phrases, passages or even experiences. Such structure can be in a variety of forms—for example, AB…BA; ABC…CBA; ABBA…ABBA; etc. See the example of the ABC structure in Samson's experience two sections above.

SAMSON X-FILE

MY THOUGHTS

PHILISTINE ADDICTION OR PUZZLING PROVIDENCE?

8

DEALING WITH DESTINY

"Let me die with the Philistines!"

Judges 16:30

Praising the Wrong god

Word of the arrest and blinding of Samson must have spread through all the cities of the Philistines like a wild fire on a very hot and windy summer day. I imagine that there was great joy and rejoicing in the dusty streets of every city. There must have been celebrative gatherings in countless Philistine homes. However, the primary center of jubilation and exultation was the temple of Dagon, the chief god of the Philistines. All of the lords from the different cities had gathered in the temple to celebrate their conquest and to offer a great sacrifice unto Dagon. These lords led the great assembly in a ceremony of antiphonal praise to their god for giving them "victory" over Samson.

As they brought Samson forward, they shouted:

"*Our god has given Samson our enemy into our hands*" (Judges 16:23). Although in their hearts they knew this was not true (for Delilah was not their god), it was socially and politically expedient for them to credit Dagon with the victory in order to mobilize the traumatized masses that were adversely affected by Samson's victorious rampage through the country. When the people saw Samson, they shouted out in response to their lords: *"Our god has given our enemy into our hands, even the destroyer of our country, who has slain many of us"* (16:24). The Philistines were praising the wrong god, and their lords knew it, but kept silent. For them, it was better for their people to praise Dagon than to acknowledge Samson's whore.

However, what these multitudes of rejoicing Philistines did not know was that while they were in high spirits offering praises to their god, Samson was praying to his, while grinding corn. In his moment of loneliness and deep despair, the great warrior found his spot with his God and plugged in to his divine power Source. In his blindness, Samson lost sight of his fatal attraction, Delilah, and began to see God again for who He was. He repented of his sin of idolatry—for giving Delilah preeminence over Jehovah—and made his peace with His Father.

Merciful Remembrance

"A broken and contrite heart, O God, you will not despise."

Psalm 51:17

> *"The righteous cry and the Lord hears, and delivers them out of all their troubles. The Lord is near to the brokenhearted, and <u>saves those who are crushed in spirit</u>."*
>
> Psalm 34:17, 18

The Lord heard the heart-cry of His downtrodden servant and remembered him. Although Samson's power supply was instantly and effectively neutralized because of the poor choice he had made, his God had not forsaken him. The author hinted this when he wrote: *However, the hair of his head began to grow again after it was shaved off* (16:22). God is always near to the brokenhearted, and ready to save those who are crushed in spirit (Psalm 34:18).

The sprouting of new hair had absolutely nothing to do with the return of Samson's power, except to indicate to the reader that it was not all over for Samson. The hair would have sprouted as a natural process of growth whether or not Samson's power had returned. The fact is that the warrior's heart was once again set right with His God. He was effectively plugged in, and the Spirit was then waiting for the right moment to *testify*. Hallelujah! (I just could not hold that one back, even if I tried.)

Rush Power V- One More Time

At the very peak of the celebration, when all the spirits of the worshippers and revelers were high (16:24), the people began to clamor for the champion, so that they could amuse themselves by making fun of him. As Samson emerged from his prison into the full view of the crowd, the people became frantic—some shouting taunts, others commands, and still others yelling curses in the name of the gods—but no one took notice of the protruding hairs on the warrior's head.

After they had had their fill of mockery of Samson, his God, and Israel, they made him stand between the pillars that supported the main structure. That was a wrong and most fatal move. When Samson perceived where he was standing, a "wild" thought raced through his brain and his muscles began to twitch involuntarily. At that very moment, Samson turned to the lad who held his hand and made what appeared to be a reasonable request. *"Let me feel the pillars on which the house rests, that I may lean against them"* (16:26).

Samson had positioned himself for his final victory, for he recognized that he was standing beneath a full house—men, women, including all the lords of the Philistines, plus over 3,000 more on the roof—and decided to bring it down to ruin. While he was leaning against the pillars of the temple, Samson's heart reached out to his *X-Factor* one more time—his second recorded conversation with his God in all of the four chapters that contains this story. This was his very simple prayer:

"O Lord GOD, <u>please remember me</u> and <u>please strengthen me just this time</u>, O God,

> *that I may at once be avenged of the Philistines for my two eyes."*
>
> Judges 16:28

Whether the Philistines heard this prayer or not, we do not know, but this man of God had a date with destiny and he was going to keep it one more time. Samson's prayer request for God to remember him was a foregone conclusion, for Christ always keeps His appointments. He had told Samson's mother that her son was going to be a Nazirite from her womb until the day of his death (Judges 13:7). This simple statement appears to have a predictive element and a promise in it, for Christ was setting a date with the unborn Samson.

Hence, when Manoah offered his sacrifice to God, Christ passed through the pieces as He ascended in the flames that consumed them (Judges 13:19-22). Through this symbolic act, Christ was covenanting with Samson's parents that as long as their son was raised and remained a Nazirite unto God, He (the angel of the Lord or Christ) was going to be with him from the time he was conceived until the day of his death. This day had come and Christ was ready to deliver on His promise.

As soon as Samson had uttered his prayer, he stepped in between the two middle pillars that supported the full house and he braced himself against them. I imagine that some of the Philistines rose to their feet to see what the deflated warrior was about to do, while others were pointing at him and scornfully laughing at his posture, just like the jeering priests around Christ's cross (Matthew 27:42).

They probably reasoned that Samson was then just like one of the regular guys, and there was no way in heaven or on earth that he could even budge those pillars. I also believe that despite all the revelry and laughter, there were many who felt tinges of fear and uneasiness, thinking that something could go terribly wrong if their leaders had underestimated Samson's strength. These fainthearted ones did not have to wait very long to see their fears materialize.

Samson shouted at the top of his lungs, as he made his very last request of God: *"Let me die with the Philistines!"* This was not the prayer of a weak, faithless, frightened man, but the war cry of a valiant Nazirite soldier, who was prepared to destroy the Philistines and settle his date with his destiny. Consequently, after sounding his battle cry, Samson pushed against those pillars with all his might, and the Spirit of Jehovah descended upon him one more time.

Before the doomed Philistines could realize what was happening, there was a loud, resounding crack. Silence reigned for a split second. Then there was grinding of stones; creaking of lumber; rumbling of concrete and piercing death screams of thousands of voices, as Samson brought down the house upon himself. In this singular, courageous act, this most misunderstood judge of Israel and warrior of the Most High, killed more Philistines on that day than in all of his 20 years fighting against them.

Samson and You

Learning to Praise

Have you ever offered praise to the wrong god for some remarkable thing that you did? I have! Me? Yes me! I have praised myself, not once or twice, but many times for my so-called outstanding achievements; and if you are honest enough, you will admit that you too have done the same. The real truth is that we often offer more praise to ourselves and others than we do offer to God.

Therefore, God sometimes allows disappointments and frustrations to come into our lives so that we can focus our thoughts on Him. Adversity and hardship inhibit us from offering our praise to the wrong god and help us readjust our thinking, so that when deliverance and breakthrough come—often in the midnight hour—we roll out our gratitude, thanksgiving and praise to the God who brought us through.

The Bible says that the Holy One inhabits (or is enthroned upon) the praises of His people, Israel (Psalm 22:3), for He delights in our praise. The Psalmist, David, says if you delight yourself in the Lord, He would give you the desires of your heart (Psalm 37:4). The offering of praise to the Almighty is the door to the blessings from His storehouse; hence the reason David made this practice a very core element of his relationship with God. I encourage you to emulate this treasured habit of this paragon of praise, who vowed:

> *I will bless the Lord at all times; His praise shall continually be in my mouth. My soul will make its boast in the LORD; The humble will hear it and rejoice.*
>
> Psalm 34:1, 2

He invites you: *O magnify the LORD with me, And let us exalt His name together* (v. 3).

God Remembers You

It is also very important to your peace and salvation that you keep in mind that God is the God of merciful remembrance. Sometimes the enemy of your souls will try to make you feel that you have gone too far for God to remember you—that you are at the point of no return; that you are beyond the pale of His saving grace. Don't you believe that suicidal lie for one moment longer! Your heavenly Father is the faithful God of merciful remembrance, and your sin cannot take you any place where His grace cannot reclaim you. For *"where sin increased, grace abounded all the more* (Romans 5:20).

God remembered Samson when he was at his lowest point, and, in doing so, displayed His willingness to remember and reclaim His rebellious people if they would turn again to Him. The Psalmist says: *"He has remembered His lovingkindness and His faithfulness to the house of Israel"* (Psalm 98:3). God will also remember you! Just call upon Him in faith and He will save you all over again!

MY THOUGHTS

9

REMEMBERING SAMSON

And what more shall I say? For time will fail me if I tell of Gideon, Barak, <u>Samson</u>, Jephthah, of David and Samuel and the prophets, ³³who by faith conquered kingdoms, performed acts of righteousness, obtained promises, shut the mouths of lions, ³⁴quenched the power of fire, escaped the edge of the sword, from weakness were made strong, became mighty in war, put foreign armies to flight.

Hebrews 11:32-34

Heaven's Hall of Faith

Today, we are surrounded by a great deal of controversy with regard to placing sports personalities in our prestigious Halls of Fame. The world of baseball, in particular, has come under extreme organizational scrutiny and public pressure for allegations of drug abuse surrounding some of its most celebrated players, who are potential candidates for its reputed Hall of Fame.

Accused persons are asked to appear before judicial councils and organizational boards in order to clear their names of any wrong-doing pertaining to their performance in various sports, so that the integrity of their personal records could be justifiably maintained. Such critical action is taken in order to retain public trust, and to hold players accountable to the fans who are important stakeholders in the entire sporting industry.

Fans would be really hurt and disappointed if they discovered that their favorite player made it to the Hall of Fame under a thick cloud of suspicion—whether by the use of performance enhancing drugs, gambling, bribery, or by any other dishonest means.

For many, many years, until now, I have struggled with the fact that Samson's name is permanently etched in the biblical record as one of God's champion examples of faith. This was rather puzzling to me. My perception concerning the character of this misunderstood warrior was already biased by all the negative images formulated through my childhood and religious acculturation.

I just could not refrain from wondering why God would place such a "rebellious," "immoral" character like Samson in His illustrious Hall of Faith, while, at the same time, offering my apologetic justifications for God's action to others who were struggling with the same question. The name of one of my favorite Bible characters, and childhood hero—even Samson—was in God's Hall of Faith, but his character remained under a cloud of suspicion. Does that sound familiar to anyone of you my readers?

David, the adulterer and murderer, was able to get past my mental filter because, I rationalized, at least he repented of his great sin, and, through that experience, produced the most profound prayer of repentance to be found in scripture. However, since Samson did not repent (at least, that's what I had thought) of his disobedience for marrying a Philistine woman, sleeping with a "high-flying" whore, or flirting around with Delilah (all Philistine women), why should he be an example of faith for me? Left to me alone, Samson would have been a "goner." He would not even have made it to the Hall, let alone to have had his name disgrace its honorable walls.

COMMENT ON HEB. 11:32-34

I know that I am not alone with this sort of reasoning. Wherever I have heard the Samson story, it has been used as a warning to teenagers (although Samson's issues were a reflection on all Israel, not just teenagers) against the following: being disrespectful and disobedient to their parents; being unequally yoked with unbelievers; immoral behavior; flirting with sin and Satan.

As important and necessary as these warnings are, they were not the main issues of Samson's story, and he was not placed in God's Hall of Faith on account of these transgressions. On the contrary, these are the very issues that would have disqualified Samson from making it to the sacred Hall for he had violated every one of them. Nevertheless, the truth that he is in Heaven's Hall of Faith means that his name has been placed there for reasons other than the warnings stated above. Although these warnings are justifiably good, we must endeavor to seek and speak the "real" truth about Samson. Let's review the unique images of this God warrior.

Samson and John the Baptist

One major truth about Samson is that he was a type of John the Baptist. His birth was miraculous, just as John's was, for the mothers of both of them were barren; but God opened their wombs for the pursuit of His sovereign purpose. Samson and John were Nazirites from the womb until the day of their deaths. The parents of both Samson and John received specific instructions with regard to the upbringing and mission of their sons.

While the angel Gabriel (Luke 1:19) appeared to John's father, Zacharias, Jesus (the angel of the Lord – Judges 13:19-22) appeared to Samson's mother (more about that later). Both Samson and John were brought into existence for a specific pre-ordained purpose—Samson, to begin the deliverance of Israel by making war with the Philistines (Judges 13:5); John, to announce the presence of the Messiah and the kingdom of heaven to Israel and the world.

Both of these men had a date with destiny. Samson was the forerunner of Samuel—the last official judge of Israel—just as John the Baptist was the forerunner of the Messiah. Notice what Christ said to Manoah's wife about her unborn son, Samson: *"he shall **begin** to deliver Israel from the hands of the Philistines"* (Judges 13:5, emphasis mine). Samson was only to begin the deliverance of Israel, and prepare the way for Samuel to finish what he started; and he did (See 1 Samuel 7:1-17). Also observe that Samuel's birth was similar to that of Samson's, for Hannah too was barren. While Samson was a Nazirite by divine election, Samuel was a Nazirite by dedication—Hannah took the Nazarite vow for her son. She said:

> *For this boy I prayed, and the LORD has given me my petition which I asked of Him. ^{28}"So I have also dedicated him to the LORD; as long as he lives he is dedicated to the LORD."*

1 Samuel 1:27, 28

Not only was Samuel appointed as a judge over Israel, he also had the more expanded role as the prophet of the Most High God. From all accounts, this faithful servant never left office—from the very day Hannah took him to the temple and placed him under Eli's tutelage—until the day of his death.

Samson and John the Baptist had much in common with each other, and both paid the ultimate price with their lives in the pursuit of heaven's purpose. There are still many Christians today who feel like John's disciples felt—that the Master could have (and should have) done something to rescue His forerunner from his "untimely," ignominious death; but John had fulfilled the purpose for which he was brought into this world. John had successfully completed his mission and on heaven's timetable it was his finest moment to exit the stage of this life as a mighty conqueror.

Jesus gave John his tribute immediately following his death. The Bible says that

> *When the messengers of John had left, He began to speak to the crowds about John, "What did you go out into the wilderness to see? A reed shaken by the wind?* ^{25} *"But what did you go out to see? A man dressed in soft clothing? Those who are splendidly clothed and live in luxury are found in royal palaces!* ^{26}*"But what did you go out to see? <u>A prophet? Yes, I say to you, and one who is more than a prophet</u>.*
>
> ^{27}*"This is the one about whom it is written, 'BEHOLD, I SEND MY MESSENGER AHEAD OF YOU, WHO WILL PREPARE YOUR WAY BEFORE YOU.'* ^{28} *"I say to you, <u>among those born of women there is no one greater than John</u>; yet he who is least in the kingdom of God is greater than he."*
>
> Luke 7:24-28

Christ also gave Samson his tribute by not only remembering him at the time of his death, but by also permanently etching his name in Heaven's Hall of Faith.

Samson and Hosea

Like Hosea, Samson was a true servant of God, who was raised up to fulfill a divine purpose. While God had chosen Hosea to dramatize Israel's whoredom with heathen nations by directing him to marry a prostitute, He used Samson not only to portray Israel's adulterous relationship with the Philistines, but also to use that relationship as grounds for the destruction of the heathen nation. In Hosea's case, God's purpose was explained, but with Samson it was implied. Samson's situation was the reverse of Israel's.

While he was joined to the Philistines in the flesh to carry out God's purpose, he was never joined to the heathen nation in spirit. Never once did the holy record state that Samson paid homage to Dagon or any other heathen god. Instead, the Bible reveals that through the power of God, Samson brought down the heathen god, destroying thousands of its lords and worshippers in the process.

The truth is that if God did not allow Hosea to give us all the behind-the-scenes information about his unequally yoked relationship—no matter how God-directed—with a practicing prostitute, we would have held Hosea suspect, just as we do Samson. Our limited comprehension of God's sovereignty and purpose would not allow us the mental accommodation to accept what is written as it is written. Judges 13:5 and 14:4 clearly indicate that God is the one who ordained the course of Samson's life.

Israel's checkered history of repeated apostasy and enslavement, and of repentance and deliverance, during the time of the judges, was reflected in Samson's ongoing engagements with Philistine women, especially his flirtatious behavior with Delilah. The God who called Hosea to spend his life in pursuit of a temple prostitute is the very same God who directed Samson to spend his life in pursuit of the Philistines. The uncomfortable truth is that heaven's agenda is not influenced by human opinions, but is set and orchestrated by divine design. God always designs His own *X-File* to suite His eternal purpose.

Samson and his Angel

Manoah said to the angel of the LORD, "What is your name, so that when your words come to pass, we may honor you?" [18]But the angel of the LORD said to him, "Why do you ask my name, seeing <u>it is wonderful?</u>". . . [22]So Manoah said to his wife, "<u>We will surely die, for we have seen God.</u>"

Judges 13:17, 18, 22

It is very interesting that the one who bore the news about Samson's birth and gave the instructions regarding his upbringing to his parents was Jesus[1] Himself—the angel of the Lord, who is called "Wonderful," Counselor, Mighty God, Everlasting Father, Prince of Peace (Isaiah 9:6). It is interesting because no where else in all the scriptures did Christ pay a personal visit to earth in order to announce the birth and development of a miracle baby. The angel Gabriel is the frequent royal ambassador bearing such great news (Luke 1:19, 26-28). However, this was not, in any way, a divine oversight or co-incidence—there is really no such thing—but rather an intentional act of the Omnipotent One who knows the end from the beginning.

Christ was the divine Watcher over the birth and life of Samson because this God-warrior was pre-ordained to foreshadow His Maker's own life-journey into human history. Samson was born to be a deliverer and a judge in order to mirror Christ's role as Savior of the world and the Judge of the same. Samson was separated unto God for the deliverance of Israel and the destruction of the Philistines. Christ was dedicated to God for the salvation of the world and the destruction of unrepentant sinners.

Prior to Samson's birth, Christ gave his mother a prophetic hint of her son's death: *"for the boy shall be a Nazirite to God from the womb to the day of his death"* (Judges 13:7). At Christ's birth, Simeon gave Mary a prophetic hint of the Messiah's death when he told her that a sword would pierce through her own bowels.

> "Behold, this <u>Child is appointed</u> for the fall and rise of many in Israel, and for a <u>sign to be opposed</u>—³⁵and <u>a sword will pierce even your own soul</u>—to the end that thoughts from many hearts may be revealed."
>
> Luke 2:34, 35

In Simeon's prophecy, he declared that Christ was appointed (pre-ordained, or pre-determined) for the fall and rise of many in Israel, for a sign to be opposed, and also to die. In the very same way Christ appointed Samson's destiny. Samson was also a sign to be opposed because no one in his time (and very few today) understood (understand) his life and its meaning. He journeyed alone, because his life was an antithesis of his culture and religious upbringing. Christ would later say: "*I have trodden the wine press alone, and from the people there was no man with Me*" (Isaiah 63:3). The rest of this verse and the three verses following it speak of Christ's vengeance against the nations.

> *I also trod them in My anger And trampled them in My wrath; And their lifeblood is sprinkled on My garments, And I stained all My raiment.* ⁴ "<u>*For the day of vengeance was in My heart*</u>*, And My year of redemption has come.* ⁵ "<u>*I looked, and there was no one to help*</u>*, And I was astonished and there was no one to uphold; <u>So My own arm brought</u>*

salvation to Me, And My wrath upheld Me. <u>⁶"*I trod down the peoples in My anger* And made them drunk in My wrath, And *I poured out their lifeblood on the earth.*"</u>

Isaiah 63:3-6

However, reflected in this very vivid description of Christ's wrath against the nations is the shadow of Samson's vengeance on the Philistines at the time of his death. He too was treading the winepress alone, for none of Israel was with him. He had taken on the Philistines single-handedly, with vengeance in his heart on account of losing his eyes (Judges 16:28). In anger, he meted out swift and terrible judgment against them, pouring out their lifeblood upon the earth.

Numbered with Transgressors

"*Let me die with the Philistines!*" (Judges 16:30)

> *For he hath made him to be sin for us, who knew no sin; that we might be made the righteousness of God in him.*

2 Corinthians 5:21

Christ became sin for us, who knew no sin. Peter said that Jesus "*Himself bore our sins in His body on the cross. . .*" (1 Peter 2:24). Samson was also the living embodiment of a sinful, rebellious nation—Israel. Everything He did in the flesh reflected what the people of Israel were actually doing in the spirit. Samson was betrayed by one very close to him for eleven hundred pieces of silver; Jesus was betrayed by His own disciple for thirty pieces of silver.

Samson was bound for the freedom of Israel, just as Christ was bound for our freedom. Samson felt the separation from God after his pandering and sin with Delilah—for the Spirit departed from him; Christ felt the separation from the Father when He bore our sins on the cross and gross darkness enshrouded Him. Samson cried out: *"O Lord God, please remember me. . ."* The Savior cried: *"My God, My God why have You forsaken Me"* (Matthew 27:46).

Christ remembered Samson and empowered Him to finish his task; the Father remembered His Son and strengthened Him to face man's last enemy. Both men had a date with death and neither could be saved from it. They both met their destiny with great confidence and resolve. One (Samson) cried: *"Let me die with the Philistines!"* The other exclaimed: *"It is finished!"* These were both prayers of acceptance and completion—acceptance of their appointed destinies, and completion of their assigned tasks.

Samson was numbered with transgressors for their destruction and Israel's deliverance; Christ was numbered with transgressors for the destruction of the rejecters of His sacrifice and deliverance and salvation for those who accept Him by faith. Just as Christ died stretched out between two sinners, Samson died stretched out between two pillars.

On the one hand, the two malefactors on the cross represented the world of sinners—those who would say, "Remember me," signifying their acceptance of salvation through faith in Jesus; and the ones who would scornfully say, "If thou be Christ, save thyself and us," signifying man's attempt to save himself (Luke 23:39-42). On the other hand, the two pillars are comparable symbols for the entire house of sinners (the Philistines and their lords) that they supported.

Finally, both Samson and Christ died outside the camp of Israel, and in their deaths both brought many more to salvation and to judgment than they did during their lifetime.

Another Suffering Servant

All these parallels between the life of Samson and Jesus are hidden gems to reward the diligent seeker after truth. We can find Christ through the life of Samson, and can also get a better understanding of Samson through the life and mission of Jesus. What a blessing! Now we can read Isaiah 53 and see not only a picture of Christ, but also vivid images of another suffering servant and warrior for God, Samson.

Let me caution you to be very careful right here, because Samson is not reflected in every verse of Isaiah 53:1-12. What we seek are glimpses, or images, of the great warrior reflected through this prophetic treatise on the life of Jesus. I have taken the liberty to underline a few verses where I believe there may be a parallel between Samson and Jesus. You may find more or even less—it really does not matter. The important thing is that you are now able to see Samson through some new spiritual lenses. Let's try it.

> <u>Who has believed our message? And to whom has the arm of the LORD been revealed</u>? ²For He grew up before Him like a tender shoot, And like <u>a root out of parched ground</u>; He has no stately form or majesty That we should look upon Him, Nor appearance that we should be attracted to Him.
>
> ³He was despised and forsaken of men, <u>A man of sorrows and acquainted with grief</u>; And like one from whom men hide their face He was despised, and <u>we did not esteem Him</u>. ⁴<u>Surely our griefs He Himself bore, And our sorrows He carried</u>; Yet we ourselves esteemed Him stricken, Smitten of God, and afflicted.
>
> ⁵But He was pierced through for our transgressions, <u>He was crushed for our iniquities</u>; The chastening for our well-being fell upon Him, And by His scourging we are healed. ⁶<u>All of us like sheep have gone</u>

<u>astray, Each of us has turned to his own way; But the LORD has caused the iniquity of us all To fall on Him.</u>

⁷<u>He was oppressed and He was afflicted, Yet He did not open His mouth;</u> Like a lamb that is led to slaughter, And like a sheep that is silent before its shearers, So He did not open His mouth. ⁸<u>By oppression and judgment He was taken away; And as for His generation, who considered That He was cut off out of the land of the living For the transgression of my people, to whom the stroke was due?</u>

⁹His grave was assigned with wicked men, Yet He was with a rich man in His death, Because He had done no violence, Nor was there any deceit in His mouth. ¹⁰<u>But the LORD was pleased To crush Him, putting Him to grief;</u> If He would render Himself as a guilt offering, He will see His offspring, He will prolong His days, And the good pleasure of the LORD will prosper in His hand.

¹¹As a result of the anguish of His soul, He will see it and be satisfied; By His knowledge the Righteous One, My Servant, will justify the many, As He will bear their iniquities. ¹²Therefore, I will allot Him a portion with the great, And He will divide the booty with the strong; <u>Because He poured out Himself</u>

to death, And was numbered with the transgressors; Yet He Himself bore the sin of many, And interceded for the transgressors.

Isaiah 53:1-12

The very first thing that caught my attention in this chapter was the opening question: *"Who could believe this report* (verse 1)? Who could believe this report about Samson after hearing (and in many cases, believing) all the negative things we have been taught about him for many years, and through many generations? Some individuals will even read this volume and still harbor negative feelings about Samson, because the report does not harmonize with their belief system.

"He grew up... like a root out of parched ground" (verse 2). The parched ground is a very powerful metaphor, and could well reflect the barren womb of Samson's mother. God birthed Samson out of barrenness. *"A man of sorrows and acquainted with grief... we did not esteem him"* (verse 3). Samson had his full share of sorrow and grief in his short life—an unfulfilled marriage of one week, betrayal by his lovers, rejection, death of his wife, torture and bondage—and we did not esteem him because we did not understand, at all, the meaning of his life. The general opinion is that Samson deserved what he got; even though what he got was symbolic of what Israel deserved. Symbolically, only symbolically, *he [Samson] bore their griefs* (verse 4) and was *crushed for their iniquities* (verse 5).

Verse 6 reflects the fact that all Israel had gone astray, and everyone did what was right in his own eyes (Judges 21:25); the iniquity of Israel was reflected in Samson life. *"By oppression and judgment* Samson *was taken away* (verse 8), clad in bronze chains, with both eyes plucked out of their sockets. Yet, when he was ridiculed, he did not complain, just like *a lamb led to the slaughter,* or *a sheep before its shearers* (verse 7). Samson had no posterity because he *was cut off out of the land of the living for the transgression of my people, to whom the stroke was due* (verse 8).

Finally, Samson *poured out himself to death, and was numbered with the transgressors*, when he allowed himself to be crushed with the Philistines on behalf of Israel. This is the Samson that I present to you my readers. May the Spirit of Jehovah, that repeatedly rushed upon this servant-warrior, rush upon you right now, and confirm this word in your heart and as He did in mind—to the glory of God, our Father.

Samson and You

Change the Picture

How you relate to the Samson of the Bible now is the critical issue. This greatly misunderstood God-warrior may have been living under a cloud of suspicion in your heart and mind for many years, probably because of your childhood memory of his story. However, having read this volume you have the opportunity, right now, to change those story-book and movie-screen images for a more biblical perspective. The record states:

> *And what more shall I say? For time will fail me if I tell of Gideon, Barak, Samson, Jephthah, of David and Samuel and the prophets, ³³who by faith conquered kingdoms, performed acts of righteousness, obtained promises, shut the mouths of lions, ³⁴quenched the power of fire, escaped the edge of the sword, from weakness were made strong, became mighty in war, put foreign armies to flight.*
>
> Hebrews 11:32-34

Truly, the story of Samson was not simply about the exploits of a great warrior—his strength and triumph or his apparent "mistakes" and "defeats"—but about God's sovereignty and providence; about the supremacy of His purpose and awesomeness of His power, the *X-Factor* in a warrior's life. In the eyes of God, Samson was just as faithful as Barak, Moses, Abraham, Gideon, Samuel or any other hall-of-faith nominee. That is why his name exists among theirs. Thank God He did not leave such selection to short-sighted men!

Ultimately, the story of Samson is a parabolic narrative of redemption and deliverance. It is a story that portrays the love of a compassionate God that was willing to redeem and deliver His people who were living in harlotry and rebellion against Him. Samson did not only mirror Israel's experience in his flesh, but was God's instrument of redemption and deliverance of His estranged people. We would miss the rich message of the Samson saga if we focus our attention only on Samson's actions and exploits and fail to see God, the *X-Factor*, at work through the life of this awesome servant and judge of Israel.

In an effort to make this issue a little more explicit, let us look at the New Testament book of the Acts of the Apostles. Really, this book is not about the exploits of Peter, James, John, Paul and the rest of the apostles (as real and important as these are). It is a book about the coming of the Holy Spirit and His powerful manifestations in the lives and experiences of these men and the believers of the early church.

In the very same way, the story of Samson is not really about him, but about the omniscient, omnipotent and omnipresent God working out his awesome purpose in, and through, His chosen vessel. Samson was God's lightning rod, His mysterious secret weapon, His active agent for the destruction of the Philistines and the deliverance of His people, Israel. It is now time for you to change your picture.

Remember the Truth

Among other things, the story of Samson is a story

of the triumph of faith. Samson was indeed a hero of faith, because it took great faith for him to choose a path that went against the norms of his life, his upbringing and his culture to pursue the path that God had chosen for him. This explicitly mirrors what Jesus did when he rejected the cultural norms, school and religious systems of His day in order to pursue His Father's plan for His life.

Samson walked a very lonely road that could not be understood by his parents, the Jewish masses then, and most Christians now, because his controversial life was the unfolding of a divine secret born in the mind of the eternal God. He trod this path alone, just as Jesus trod the winepress alone (Isaiah 63:3).

Only the Master, who chose Samson to accomplish His purpose, truly understood the life of His servant, because He too lived that life. Hence, because of His faithfulness and love, Christ did not allow His servant to become a defenseless victim, tried in the court of popular public (and even Christian) opinion, or to be regarded as a suspicious, questionable character throughout biblical history.

The Angel of the Lord, whose name is Wonderful (Judges 13:18, compare Isaiah 9:6), most certainly did not permit the sacred record to close without first reserving a place for His obedient servant in His Hall of Faith. In his Master's heart, Samson was a faithful hero, not a fallen villain. This is how God remembers His chosen warrior and so should you. Therefore, you need to change your picture and your story. Proclaim the "real" truth about

Samson, and about God—Samson's *X-Factor*. Will you?

Notes:

1. See chapter one for the explanation with regard to the angel of the Lord.

REMEMBERING SAMSON

MY THOUGHTS

SAMSON X-FILE

ABOUT THE AUTHOR

Ruthven J. Roy is a native of Trinidad and Tobago, W.I. He has been a teacher and a preacher of the Word of God for over 33 years. As the founder and president of Network Discipling Ministries, Dr. Roy has spent many years in the Caribbean, the United States and Canada, teaching and training thousands of believers how to become contagious, fruit-bearing disciples of Christ.

Dr. Roy completed his undergraduate studies in Theology at the University of the Southern Caribbean. Later, he received his graduate degrees—a Master of Divinity and Doctor of Ministry—at Andrews University, Michigan. He also obtained his Masters in Business Administration at Western Michigan University. He and his wife, Lyris, have three grown daughters, Charisa, Lyrisa and Mirisa.

More Exciting Titles
by Dr. Ruthven J. Roy

Imitating God

Imitating God is not only possible, but it is also guaranteed. This book will make available to you the key to your true identity, and will show you, in very simple steps, how to unleash the power of God's life from within you. Get ready to enter into the **God-zone**.

ISBN: 978-0-9717853-3-5

The Explosive Power of Network Discipling

"Every Christian is called to be a disciple of Jesus; and every disciple is called to be a fisher, not just a member!" In this volume Dr. Roy clearly explains Christ's master plan for growing His kingdom. Christ calls everyone to discipleship, not membership.

ISBN: 978-0-9717853-4-2

MORE EXCITING TITLES

Study Guide: Imitating God

Do not forget this companion Study Guide to go along with this magnificent text. It would greatly enhance your understanding of all the vital issues that pertain to your spiritual identity and living victoriously. Moreover, this Study Guide will provide you with an exciting, hands-on way to share this good news with others.

ISBN: 978-0-9717853-6-6

Available at your local Christian bookstore

For more information, visit www.networkdiscipling.org, or write to Rehoboth Publishing, P.O. Box 33, Berrien Springs, MI 49103

Contact Information

*NETWORK DISCIPLING MINISTRIES
P.O. Box 33
Berrien Springs, MI 49103*

Tel: (301) 514-2383
Email: ruthvenroy@gmail.com
Website: www.networkdiscipling.org

www.ingramcontent.com/pod-product-compliance
Lightning Source LLC
LaVergne TN
LVHW040116080426
835507LV00039B/386